A Macrotheory of Justice

A Macrotheory of Justice

A Response to Contemporary Theories of Justice

GABRIEL MSOKA

WIPF & STOCK · Eugene, Oregon

A MACROTHEORY OF JUSTICE
A Response to Contemporary Theories of Justice

Copyright © 2011 Gabriel Msoka. All rights reserved. Except for brief quotations in critical publications or reviews, no part of this book may be reproduced in any manner without prior written permission from the publisher. Write: Permissions, Wipf and Stock Publishers, 199 W. 8th Ave., Suite 3, Eugene, OR 97401.

Wipf & Stock
An Imprint of Wipf and Stock Publishers
199 W. 8th Ave., Suite 3
Eugene, OR 97401
www.wipfandstock.com

ISBN 13: 978-1-60899-834-0

Manufactured in the U.S.A.

This work is dedicated to all those who do justice to humankind, God, and nature.

Contents

List of Abbreviations • ix
Introduction • xi

PART 1: Exposition and Critique of Justice Theories
Introduction • 1
1 Justice, Liberalism, and Feminism • 3
2 Justice and Utilitarianism • 20
3 Justice and Libertarianism • 30
4 Justice and Communitarianism • 39
   Part 1 Conclusion • 48

PART 2: Possible Sources for Constructing a Macrotheory of Justice
Introduction • 49
5 African Cultural Narratives of Justice • 51
6 Biblical Narratives of Justice • 61
   Part 2 Conclusion • 75

PART 3: Towards a Paradigmatic Theory of Justice
Introduction • 77
7 The Ethical and Moral Significance of a Macrotheory of Justice • 79
8 Methodological Considerations for Constructing a Macrotheory of Justice • 93
   General Conclusion • 127

Bibliography • 129

List of Abbreviations

AFER	*African Ecclesial Review*
AMECEA	Association of Member Episcopal Conferences in Eastern Africa
Cosmotheandrism	Interrelation of cosmos (nature), theos (God), anthropos (humankind)
JB	Jerusalem Bible
MPLA	Movimento Popular de Libertação de Angola (Popular Movement for the Liberation of Angola)
ORUM	Kichagga version of cosmotheandrism: oruka (nature), rua (God), mdu (humankind)
UMUMTU	Kiswahili version of cosmotheandrism: ulimwengu (nature), mungu (God), mtu (humankind)
UNITA	União Nacional para a Independência Total de Angola (National Union for the Total Independence of Angola)

Introduction

The modern discourses on justice have not gone far enough in addressing the critical issues of justice and injustices facing not only humankind[1] but also nature.[2] By and large, the theories have often confined the notion of justice or injustice to one area, i.e., humankind. The liberal view of justice, for example, focuses on a fair way to enjoy or distribute equal rights and duties in human society (equality of the individual person). The libertarian view of justice focuses on enjoying or exercising individual liberty or freedom to make personal decisions, acquire and exchange goods with someone else, or make contracts or agreements (commutative justice). These two contemporary theories, as well as the theories of feminism, classical utilitarianism, and communitarianism will be examined in their methods of justice, principles of justice, and in their application.

Moreover, the sacred and spiritual character of humankind and nature has not been considered as integral to the contemporary theories of justice, as the macrotheory of justice will demonstrate. Two major areas will be examined as possible sources for constructing a macrotheory of justice: biblical narratives of justice, *sedaqah*, and African narratives of justice, *UMUMTU*. From the biblical perspective the term *justice*, or *sedaqah*, is interpreted as fidelity to the demands of the covenantal relationship with God (Yahweh). Thus, as an expression of such a relationship, a just person or social system is judged by the way the most vulnerable groups, such as the poor, the orphan, the widow, and the stranger, are treated or protected. It is worth noting, however, that African cultural narratives of justice are broader than the biblical narratives of justice.

---

1. In the study of macrojustice, the term *humankind* is inclusive and applies to both man and woman. It also applies to the living dead (ancestors) as well as those not yet born. The spiritual aspect of humankind is also considered. Many contemporary theories of justice, however, confine the term *humankind* to persons living only in the physical world and exclude the spiritual world, the ancestors (the living dead) and the unborn.

2. The term nature (cosmos) applies to animate (the living: animals and plants) and inanimate beings (nonliving).

From the African perspectives, the terms for justice, UMUMTU and ORUM, are interpreted not only as the right relationship with humankind and God, as the biblical justice, *sedaqah*, emphasizes, but also the right relationship with nature. In Africa, the concept of justice has three components: humankind, God, and nature. Justice as the right relationship with humankind, God, and nature is critical to the study of the macrotheory of justice, which was not under any consideration in the study of the contemporary theories of justice.

This book has three parts and eight chapters. Part 1 exposes and critiques the theories of liberalism, libertarianism, feminism, classical utilitarianism, and communitarianism. Chapters 1, 2, 3, and 4 analyze the above theories in depth and expose their strengths and flaws. Part 2 suggests the possible sources for constructing a macrotheory of justice. Chapter 5 describes the nature and scope of the African cultural narratives of justice, UMUMTU and ORUM. Chapter 6 describes the nature and scope of the biblical narratives of justice by examining a number of passages from both the Old and the New Testaments. Part 3 proposes a paradigmatic theory of justice. Chapter 7 discusses the ethical and moral significance of a macrotheory of justice by critically examining the Catholic interpretation and application of biblical justice. Chapter 8 offers a methodological consideration for constructing a macrotheory of justice.

By developing a macrotheory of justice, we can achieve a better and deeper understanding that:

1. It is a sacred duty and a priority to protect nature, and therefore, it is not an option.

2. Committing injustices against nature is unethical and immoral.

3. Integral peace is a result of right relationship with humankind, God, and nature.

4. Doing justice toward humankind and nature is tantamount to doing justice toward God.

Part 1

Exposition and Critique of Justice Theories

For too long a time, contemporary theories of justice have been focusing on the human person as the sole bearer of justice, and too little has been done regarding nature or cosmos, the bearer of justice in its own right. Part 1 examines the nature and scope of social theories of liberalism, libertarianism, feminism, classical utilitarianism, and communitarianism, reconstructing the theories of justice and presenting a critical assessment of each theory's method, principles of justice, and their application, by identifying their strengths and limitations. Chapter 1 examines justice, liberalism, and feminism; chapter 2 examines justice and classical utilitarianism; chapter 3 examines justice and libertarianism; and chapter 4 examines justice and communitarianism.

1 Justice, Liberalism, and Feminism

EXPOSITION OF THE THEORIES

The question now is: what is feminism? Some people tend to think that feminism and lesbianism are one and the same thing. Because of this connection, feminism has often been misunderstood and viewed with a lot of suspicion. Actually, feminism is a social theory that addresses the issues of justice related to women in the world. As a women's movement, feminism has evolved into many forms, such as liberal feminism, social feminism, Marxist feminism, bioethical feminism, Christian feminism, African feminism, and others. Despite these variations, they all share one commonality, namely the emancipation of women. Among the forms of feminism mentioned, this chapter will include discussions of Western liberal feminism, bioethical feminism, social feminism, and African feminism.

Feminism and liberalism are not the same, but is there anything in common between the two theories? Historically, liberal feminism was an offshoot of the liberal tradition of Western society and culture, particularly at the turn of the nineteenth century. Prior to these changes, liberalism and feminism shared common goals, values, and visions, such as liberty, individual dignity, and equal opportunity.[1] Despite this commonality, there emerged a huge chasm between liberal feminism and classic liberalism. Liberal feminism rejects so-called abstract individualism,[2] a classical liberal system of thought that ignores equal social opportunity for women by encouraging the dichotomy between the domestic and public domains. Liberal feminists maintain that what is domestic ought to be public and that bridging the two domains is a matter of justice.

The struggle for justice in feminism is to achieve women's liberation from oppression in a gender-structured society. As the traditional

---

1. Segers, "Feminism, Liberalism, and Catholicism," 249.
2. Ibid., 250.

gender structure of society confines women to domestic domain, less and less women have been able to participate in the public life. Therefore, as a movement, feminism seeks ways to liberate women from all forms of oppression with a view to establishing gender equality in both domestic and public domains.

Even as late as the 1930s, feminism was ill perceived by many men and women alike on the continent of Africa. As Patricia McFadden puts it:

> For a while, African women who named themselves "feminists" were looked upon as "disloyal" by both women and men who consciousness had been shaped and oriented through nationalist ideology and old notions of authenticity and difference. It was "un-African" to be feminist, let alone name oneself thus.[3]

However, as time passed by, it drew some public sympathy and support. Still, others viewed the feminist struggle as a woman's problem that had nothing to do with the rest in the society. Furthermore, the majority of men and even some women interpreted liberal feminism as a strange doctrine and viewed it with great suspicion; it appeared to be a theory that could pose a serious threat to men's world, a stepping stone to a coup d'état of the cultural establishment. Nevertheless, in the course of time and due to public pressure, the movement gained a great momentum and began to take roots. Consequently, feminism gained a considerable support from the public.

Right from the start, feminist thinkers sought to address crucial factors that have contributed to the oppression of women in the Western world: the interpretation and application of religion, culture, and biotechnology to different domains of life. To address the fundamental rights of women, feminism calls for gender equality in both domestic and public life. Feminism attempts to bridge the domestic and public domains by maintaining that whatever is domestic is also public.

In the following sections, I will present the ideas of a variety of feminist thinkers. Cristina Traina, an ethicist and feminist, highlights feminism from the perspective of religion. Traina claims that the interpretation of natural law in the Catholic Church has been, and still is, the domain of a few. Consequently, the majority of the church members, including women, have been excluded from this process. Therefore, Traina argues

---

3. McFadden, "Feminism in Africa Today," para. 4.

that there is a need to have in place the procedural inclusion of women in interpreting the natural law. Susan Moller Okin, a liberal feminist, and Iris Marion Young, a social feminist, both highlight and connect the concepts of culture, oppression, and feminism from the Western perspective. Mercy Amba Oduyoye, an African Christian feminist, interprets feminism from the African religion and culture. From the bioethical feminist perspective, Margaret Farley and Rosemarie Tong highlight the subject. By learning from these different thinkers, we will expose the strengths and weaknesses of feminism.

FEMINISM AND RELIGION

Cristina Traina defines feminism as "a practical and intellectual dedication to the discovery and uprooting of ideological relationships, and institutions that thwart women's creation of new ideologies, relationships and institutions that promote it."[4] She suggests that natural law, a medieval European philosophy that determines the moral norms and goals of human actions, offers a method to pursue feminist goals. However, Traina also holds the view that the interpretation of natural law was the domain of a few people within the Catholic tradition:

> The failure of this majority to influence the official Roman Catholic ethical conversation is due less to incompatibility of their ideas with natural law theory—which is *methodologically* open to all new evidence about the human—than to the *procedural* exclusion from the community that makes normative moral judgments.[5]

Traina further claims that such exclusion "incapacitates natural law's methodological openness to new information and eventually profoundly distorts both its content and its conduct."[6]

Lisa Cahill shares similar views with Traina:

> Women and men share one human nature and . . . whatever their functional biological differences are, the exaggerated gender roles that have separated them historically, the commonality of that nature warrants similar moral treatment.[7]

---

4. Traina, *Feminist Ethics and Natural Law*, 25.
5. Ibid., 145.
6. Ibid., 145.
7. Cahill, "Feminism and Christian Ethics," 216.

Traina argues that communal participation in public moral discourse is crucial to women's moral development and maturity, adding that such a development contributes to everyone's well-being. Traina insists that solidarity with women is good for all of humanity. In order to advance the course for feminist ethics, there is a need to involve both the oppressed and the oppressors in the liberation process.[8] Traina notes, "The meaning and content of the moral norms must be adequate to women's critically interpreted moral experience."[9] Traina argues that feminist interpretation should include not only "the theoretical freedom to do as [they] please, but also the prerequisites for truly free choices including healthy bodies, healthy relationships, and a degree of economic and political security."[10] Feminist and natural law ethicists "embrace the turn to the subject, personalist criteria for moral norms, a creed of individual dignity."[11] As in the natural law tradition, "feminist accounts of women's flourishing embrace not only individual physical health, but also intellectual, psychological, and spiritual flourishing in the interdependent community."[12]

Basically, epistemology of experience is a starting point for both feminist and natural law ethics.[13] At this juncture, Traina outlines some specific areas of shared understanding between feminists and natural law ethics. First, virtue is understood as a "habit of right discernment and action, not merely the ability to make isolated 'good decisions.'"[14] Second, "reason" is the engagement with practical reason—the reason involved when we decide how to act—as opposed to theoretical reason. Third, "common good" involves individual integral and participation in social structures. Fourth, "ethical reflection" is shaped by our social connection.[15] Traina also admits the fact that "feminism is a coherent set of critical and constructive tools, and not a comprehensive moral theory."[16] Finally, Traina insists that authentic feminist ethics requires us to "adopt telic anthropology" with its guidelines for organizing and choosing

8. Traina, 147.
9. Ibid.
10. Ibid.
11. Ibid., 150.
12. Ibid., 151.
13 Ibid., 154–55.
14. Ibid., 155.
15. Ibid., 155–57.
16. Ibid., 159.

among goods. One credible telos is a version of natural law's final end, union with God, which Traina believes can be positive contribution to feminist ethics.[17]

Critique

First, Christina Traina's interpretation of feminist ethics places women's experiences at the center of moral discourse and moral flourishing. Traina argues in favor of "preferential option for the women" while at the same time, trying to avoid exclusive feminist ethics by asserting that women's liberation is for the well-being of all, namely, for both the oppressors and the oppressed. Second, Traina values the importance of developing an inclusive and participatory approach in doing ethics. Third, Traina also acknowledges the level of cooperation that can be developed between the natural law tradition and feminism. Since "epistemological experience" is a starting point both for feminist and natural law ethicists, Traina argues that there is some light at the end of the "tunnel" for feminists to develop some conversation with natural law ethicists.[18] The weakness in Traina's view of feminism is that feminism can be separate from the natural law tradition. Feminist ethics, as Traina conceives it, must yet develop its own distinctive method, content, and principles instead of depending entirely on natural law tradition.

FEMINISM, BIOTECHNOLOGY, AND BIOETHICS

Margaret Farley, a feminist ethicist and theologian, believes that women's bodies play a very crucial role in biotechnology. Farley holds what may seem to be a shocking position and an extreme view, namely that biotechnology is a source of women's oppression, and so she uses theological and ethical reflection to call for women's liberation:

> Whatever else feminist theology does, it proceeds from a methodological focus on the experience of women, and whatever feminist ethics does, it begins with a central concern for the well-being of women.[19]

---

17. Ibid., 158–59.
18. Farley, "Feminist Theology and Bioethics," 192.
19. Ibid., 192.

With this notion, Farley hopes to establish a connection between feminist theology and issues in the field of bioethics,[20] and how they can affect the lives of women.

Farley holds that feminist theology and ethics start with concrete objective reality, namely women's experiences of oppression.[21] Farley claims that patterns of relation, patterns of embodiment, and patterns within the world of nature have had an impact on bioethics. Since these have contributed to the oppression of women, Farley believes that there is a need for a new understanding and interpretation in bioethical issues geared towards the liberation of women.[22] Also, for the women's liberation to become a reality, Farley argues that feminist ethics demands a "feminist hermeneutical principle which functions in the selection and interpretation of all other sources."[23]

Farley notes that some feminists have claimed that the "psychological capability of bearing children" is the ultimate source of women's oppression.[24] Farley cites Shulamith Firestone, who maintains this pattern of thought:

> Freeing of women from the tyranny of their reproductive biology by every means available, including technology could separate women once and for all from a gender-identified responsibility for reproduction.[25]

Yet Farley also believes that childbearing is not only the source of oppression but it is also a source of joy and fulfillment for women.[26]

With regard to in vitro fertilization, Farley argues that although fertilization has contributed to women's alienation and that it should occasion grave moral caution, it has also caused a sigh of relief to infertile women. Farley cautions that the use of reproductive techniques must be left to the decision of the parties concerned.[27] Rosemarie Tong, a bioethicist, shares a similar moral concern on the limited accessibility of such

---

20. Ibid.
21. Ibid., 102.
22. Ibid., 196–200.
23. Ibid., 202.
24. Ibid., 204.
25. Ibid., 205.
26. Ibid.
27. Ibid., 206.

techniques to people and whether the state could provide such services to both rich and poor alike.[28] Farley makes two cautionary notes with regard to in vitro fertilization: (1) women will be subjected to "collectivism" or state control that would eventually bring about "total alienation of one's life to institutions external to one's own control and governed by a managerial elite,"[29] and (2) selection of offspring can pose some difficulty with regard to a belief that some feminists see it as eroding morals and religious obligations to accept all sorts of persons into the human community. Farley further argues that such an attitude "undermines the basic feminist principles of equality, inclusiveness, mutuality, tolerance of difference and of imperfection."[30]

Finally, Farley concludes by saying that there is a need to evaluate in vitro fertilization according to "norms of justice." In Farley's view, the morality of in vitro fertilization must be judged not only in the context of reproductive techniques and scientific curiosity, but also in the context of the integral well-being of a child; basic human needs including human relationships are crucial in considering the morality of in vitro fertilization.[31]

Critique

Farley underscores three points on the subject of feminist ethics: first, she has demonstrated that women's experience of oppression is a methodological principle in feminist theology and ethics. Second, she has successfully pointed out both the positive and negative impacts of in vitro fertilization. Third, she has demonstrated that biotechnology needs bioethics to protect the interests both of women and of children from some form of exploitation. As Rosemarie Tong notes, "compared to men, women ordinarily have to accept not only more physical intrusions into their own bodies but also more responsibility for their ultimate fate of their embryos."[32]

---

28. Tong, *Feminist Approach to Bioethics*, 232–33, 240.
29. Farley, "Feminist Theology and Bioethics," 207.
30. Ibid., 208.
31. Ibid., 208–9.
32. Tong, *Feminist Approach to Bioethics*, 321.

However, as also Tong notes, there is a possibility that biotechnology might condone sexism and racism.[33] Feminist bioethicists perceive the idea that, in the course of creating a perfect society through the modern techniques, there might be a danger that the so-called imperfect people might be discriminated against by society and that some form of condemnation might be extended to those who brought them in the world, especially those faced with limited options.

FEMINISM, CULTURE, AND LIBERALISM

This section discusses feminism and culture from two perspectives: first, feminism from the Euro-American cultural perspective, and second, from the perspective of African culture and religion. Renowned feminists Iris Marion Young (a social constructionist feminist) and Susan Moller Okin (a liberal feminist) will highlight the discussion and reflection on feminism vis-à-vis Euro-American culture. Young and Okin will also offer a critique of liberalism. Mercy Amba Oduyoye will be the chief proponent of feminism from an African perspective.

Liberalism and Culture

Iris Marion Young is one the outstanding modern feminists of our century. Young believes that culture is one of the greatest factors that has contributed to the oppression of women in the Euro-American world.

Young's reflection on this topic was mainly motivated by the writings of a liberal social theorist, John Rawls. In *A Theory of Justice*, John Rawls maintains that in order to have in place fair principles of justice in society, there is a need to formulate such principles behind the veil of ignorance through the method of original position.[34] In the veil of ignorance of the hypothetical situation, one would not consider one's economic or political position in society so as to formulate principles of justice that were fair for all.[35] The method serves an important purpose with respect to resolving certain discrepancies or even doubtful judgments. This approach ensures that the principles chosen match our considered convictions of justice or extend them in an acceptable way.[36] Judgments reached in the original

33. Ibid., 241.
34. Rawls, *Theory of Justice*, 118.
35. Ibid.
36. Ibid., 17.

position serve as "provisional fixed points which we presume any conception of justice must fit."[37]

Rawls recognizes the fact that certain difficulties must be resolved by taking a fresh look at whether judgments coincide with one's principles or not. This is a back and forth movement. This state of affairs is known as *reflective equilibrium*. Rawls calls it equilibrium because he believes that "the principles and judgment" will eventually coincide; and it is reflective since "we know to what principles of our judgment conform and the premises of their derivation."[38] Despite the fact that this approach serves a very practical purpose in resolving certain situations, he also admits that reflective equilibrium is "not necessarily stable" and therefore further scrutiny could be employed as needed.[39] At this stage, Rawls seems content with the state of affairs with regard to our convictions of social justice and that a conception of the original position has finally been reached.[40]

The principles of justice that the original position describes are as follows: first, "each person is to have an equal right to the most extensive scheme of equal basic liberty rights compatible with a similar scheme of liberties for others. Second, social and economic inequalities are to be arranged so that they are both (a) reasonably expected to be at every one's advantage, and (b) attached to positions open to all."[41] As regards the application of the principles of justice, Rawls examines three kinds of procedural justice: perfect procedural justice, imperfect procedural justice, and pure procedural justice. Perfect procedural justice is that in which there exists an independent criterion for deciding which outcome is just and a procedure guaranteed to lead to it. Imperfect procedural justice is that in which there is an independent criterion but the procedure does not necessarily yield the desired results. Finally, pure procedural justice is that in which there is no independent criterion in reference to the determination of the right results but the correct procedure will eventually yield the correct results provided that such a procedure has been correctly been followed.[42] Rawls opts for pure procedural justice simply to ensure

37. Ibid., 18.
38. Ibid.
39. Ibid.
40. Ibid.
41. Ibid., 54.
42. Ibid., 74–75.

that his theory would yield best results, adding that the principles chosen behind the veil of ignorance yield principles of justice that are fair.

Feminist Critique of Liberalism

Young focuses her critique on Rawls's principles of distributive justice in the original position, whose paradigm of moral reasoning detaches universality from particularity. Young argues that justice requires "not principles that apply to all people in the same way, but a nuanced understanding of the particularity of the social context."[43] Young is convinced that the ideal of impartiality generates a dichotomy between universal and particular and that particularities are part of the moral reasoning.[44] Young then argues that the dichotomy between the public and domestic has to be eliminated.

On the one hand, Rawls still believes that parties at the original position would still have to know certain facts of life about human society that would affect the choice of the principles. On the other hand, Rawls maintains, "No one knows his place in society, his class position or social status."[45] In such a case, Young believes that this approach denies or represses differences.[46] Young also criticizes postmodern philosophers such as Theodor Adorno (1973) and Jacques Derrida (1977) who attempted to repress differences to reconstruct the so-called the logic of identity.[47] Young notes, "The logic of identity also seeks to reduce the plurality of particular subjects, their bodily, perspectival experience, to a unity, by measuring them against the varying standard of universal reason."[48]

It is therefore within this philosophical framework that dichotomies developed and finally got into the general public. These dichotomies in Western discourse are structured by the dichotomy between good/bad, pure/impure, subject/object, mind/body, and nature/culture.[49] Reason was associated with masculinity, while body, desire, and affectivity was closely related to femininity. The notion of women being associated with

---

43. Young, *Politics of Difference*, 96.
44. Ibid., 97.
45. Rawls, *Theory of Justice*, 118–19.
46. Young, *Politics of Difference*, 98.
47. Ibid.
48. Ibid., 90.
49. Ibid.

the body and desire as opposed to reason became embedded in civic public. This notion was highly advocated and supported by Rousseau, who believed that femininity was associated with sentiment and desire while masculinity was associated with reason. Consequently, women were confined to marriage and to domestic domain. The notion of reason was also associated with race, such that citizenship was restricted to white men on the ground that the unity of nation depended on homogeneity and dispassionate reason.[50]

Contrary to Rawls's notion of abstract citizens behind the veil of ignorance, Young argues that a communicative ethics that recognizes the plurality of subjects would be more appropriate.[51] Young believes that the idea of impartiality serves three ideological purposes: First, it supports the idea of the neutral state, which in turn provides grounds for the distributive paradigm of justice. Second, it legitimates bureaucratic authority and a hierarchical decision-making process. Third, it reinforces oppression by hypostatizing the point of view of privileged groups into a universal position.[52] Young then argues that the ideal of a neutral state that stands above the particular interests and conflicts of civil society is a Marxist ideal. Young maintains that being fair does not require stepping out of one's skin.[53] While bureaucratic authority and a hierarchical decision-making process may serve ideological ends, Young advocates its justification as long as positions are assigned impartially according to merit, and that democracy may be unnecessary as long as decision makers strive for impartiality.[54] Young also points out that the ideal of impartiality generates a propensity to universalize the particular especially where "positions of decision making authority are usually occupied by members of privileged groups.[55] As regards Rawls's original position, Young advocates participatory democracy. Young concludes her critique of Rawls by arguing that people's needs be expressed in their particularity in the heterogeneous public.[56]

50. Ibid., 111.
51. Ibid., 106.
52. Ibid., 112.
53. Ibid., 114.
54. Ibid., 115.
55. Ibid., 116.
56. Ibid., 121.

Based on the critique of Rawls's theory of justice and others, Young proposes a number of measures to bridge the domestic/personal and the public/political. First, instead of the hypothetical contract that Rawls seems to propose in his original position, there should be concrete and real people considered in their contexts. This alternative approach will give rise to communicative ethics that will eventually respect the totality of each individual's decisions. Second, this inductive method proposed will eventually collapse the dichotomy between public and private. Third, while Young seeks to bridge the private with the public, she is of the view that participatory democracy would promote the ideal of the heterogeneous public against the homogeneity of the so-called enlightenment republicanism.[57]

As stated earlier, Rawls's theory of justice focuses on "the basic structure of society, or more exactly the way in which the major social institutions distribute fundamental rights and duties, and determine the division of advantages from social cooperation."[58] For Susan Moller Okin, the question of sex and gender is critical for feminist ethics. With respect to Rawls's method of original position in which principles of justice are chosen behind the veil of ignorance, Okin observes that not only was inclusive language not used but also the question of sex was ignored.[59] Okin thinks that this veil of ignorance should be lifted to let differences of the individual parties be laid open. Okin also claims that although Rawls did include family as one of the basic structures of society, he did not give the emphasis it deserves. Okin argues that family justice is crucial on account that family is "the first school of moral development."[60] In the same vein, Okin raises the question of gender differences within families, and she believes that the difference can easily hinder development of women and girls in particular and that an alternative way should be found to advocate for gender equality.

Okin further claims that in the United States nearly 25 percent of children are being raised in single female–headed households, which include three-fifths of all chronically poor households with children. Many millions of children of both sexes are directly affected by the higher rate

---

57. Ibid., 119.
58. Rawls, *Theory of Justice*, 6.
59. Okin, *Justice, Gender, and the Family*, 91.
60. Ibid., 94.

of poverty among such families.[61] Division of labor according to gender has a serious impact in the development of children:

> Opportunities of females are significantly affected by the structures and practice of gendered family life, particularly by the fact that women are almost invariably primary caretakers, which has much impact on their availability for full-time wage-work, results in their frequently being over-worked and renders them less likely than men to be considered economically valuable.[62]

Okin believes that this situation faces both rich and poor countries alike:

> Women who provide the sole economic support for their families often face particular hardships. Discrimination against women in access to jobs, pay, retention, and promotion are common to most countries, with obviously deleterious effects on female-supported families. Many such women in both rich and poor countries also suffer from severe time-poverty, since they are carrying the double burden of domestic and breadwinning responsibilities.[63]

In an effort to confront this situation head-on, Okin recommends that there should be in place an effective public policy to provide gender equality in society. This approach may be possible on the condition that "fully human moral or political theory can be developed only with full participation of both sexes."[64]

Feminism and African Culture

Mercy Amba Oduyoye, a feminist Christian theologian, presents an African perspective of feminism. Oduyoye thinks that feminism should include all people. "What is called 'feminist theology,' then, is the theology of women and men who acknowledge and subscribe to a conscious application of their experiences in reflection."[65] Like many of Oduyoye's Western counterparts, she starts from women's voices and experiences of oppression and impoverishment and moves to liberation and flourishing.[66] Unlike the Western world, Oduyoye believes that there are two

61. Okin, "Inequalities between the Sexes," 282.
62. Ibid.
63. Ibid., 283.
64. Okin, *Justice, Gender and the Family*, 107.
65. Oduyoye, "Feminist Theology in an African Perspective," 166–67.
66. Ibid., 167.

areas of major concern common to both men and women theologians in Africa: First, there is the question of marginalization from the global technological culture; exploitation that results from unjust global trade and economic arrangements is a significant area for some African theologians, including both men and women. Second, the theology of African traditional religion and culture is the most appropriate subject for addressing feminism.[67] The latter seems to Oduyoye the most crucial aspect worth considering in the African feminist theology scholarship because culture and religion play a crucial role in Africa. Then, Oduyoye singles out marriage and procreation as critical for understanding an African feminist theology. For Oduyoye, sexuality, marriage, and procreation are closely connected. In the Western world, sexuality, marriage, and procreation are at times dissociated from each other such that sexuality outside marriage and procreation can be a legitimate personal moral experience. In other words, romantic love is seen as the best manner of expressing meaningful sexuality between a couple. Hence, sex is often for recreation rather than for procreation. Oduyoye supports the traditional African view of sex as dependent on marriage and procreation, but she nevertheless takes aim at her own home by challenging the factors that contribute to women's oppression in Africa.

> African women, whether born to matriarchal or patriarchal families, are expected to use strength they have to protect and not to destroy. But women are ready for destruction if that would mean life for community. Their very imputed strength is turned to weakness. Women continue to observe taboos that place them at a disadvantage in economic, social, and political life.[68]

Not all forms of feminism are good for Africa. Oduyoye presents a number of useful tools for a reconstruction of African feminism:

1. African women should explore traditional matriarchal values to determine which aspects might be woven into new forms of relations between men and women.[69]
2. Women need to present mothering as a positive strategy for community life that is to be practiced by all women and all men.[70]

67. Ibid.
68. Ibid., 172.
69. Ibid., 176.
70. Ibid.

3. Reciprocity in life giving and caring in both women and men can work against some negative forms of patriarchalization of life.[71]

In order to construct an African feminist theology, Oduyoye believes that there is a need to employ a Christian anthropology that would enrich the understanding of sexuality for both men and women as cocreators with God.[72] For Oduyoye, there is a close link between sexuality and procreation, and she argues that sexuality and procreation are inseparable. Oduyoye underscores the importance for "women to apply themselves to serious study to forge a theology of marriage."[73] Sexuality should be an issue to be faced within African Christianity as an integral part of our understanding of the human body and human person.[74] Finally, women's biblical scholarship is an essential component to reconstruct a theology of liberation in Africa.[75]

Critique

Is feminism feasible in Africa? Is so, why and how? If not, why? From the preceding discussions, there seems to be an impression that feminism deals with women's liberation without requiring an involvement of men. Referring to Traina's remarks, it appears that for any success in this endeavor, the liberation process must involve both the oppressor and the oppressed. Before feminist literature came to my knowledge in 2003, I was quite skeptical about the aim and the objective of this movement. Furthermore, I even thought that feminism was some sort of a weird and strange social doctrine associated with lesbianism, which would cause social friction and confrontation between men and women in Africa. If this were the case, then feminism would be persona non grata on the African soil. Oduyoye argues quite the opposite and offers the continent some hope for the possibility of an African feminism. Before this happens, Oduyuye argues that there is a need to reconstruct a meaningful African feminist theology by retrieving from the African culture and religion the values of matriarchy, mothering, sexuality, and the reciprocity in giving,

---

71. Ibid., 176–77.
72. Ibid., 178.
73. Ibid., 179.
74. Ibid.
75. Ibid.

caring, and nurturing. This study can be enhanced by a Christian anthropology that interprets both men and women as cocreators with God.

Both Western and African forms of feminism focus on women's experience of oppression as the common denominator. In both of these perspectives, culture has been cited by the both approaches as one of the major sources of oppression of women.

Western feminists have also been preoccupied with the question of the relationship between feminism and bioethics, as Tong's reflections have shown. Since biotechnology uses women's bodies for experiments, and intrudes on their privacy, women in the Western world are seeking autonomy in the decisions affecting their lives and well-being. While biotechnology has already been seen as a form of oppression for women, feminism has also been seen as critical for women's liberation.

Oduyoye talks about the issue of biotechnology, but she hardly develops it. In the face of globalization, the impact of technology in Africa is something that should not be ignored. Despite the positive aspects that globalization brings to our modern society, the dark side should also be taken seriously. Robert J. Schreiter explains the impact of globalization: "Globalization not only extends the effects of modernity and with it elements of Western culture. It has a compressing effect as well."[76] In other words, globalization deals with compression of time and space, and therefore the effects of modernity become extended across the globe. Whether or not African women, like Oduyoye, are enthusiastic about the dawn of biotechnology, the fact of the matter is that modern technology is inevitable. The issue that needs to be addressed here is how best technology can be instrumental in promoting the integral well-being of people in Africa.

African women intelligentsia including academics, researchers, and others have to collectively brace for the battle that the impact of modern biotechnology continues to pose on the African continent. African women have already started to employ the language of women's rights to reproductive health and autonomy in decision making regarding what is good for their lives.

While there is a move by some women to free women from the so-called reproductive tyranny in the name of autonomy, there is also a feeling by other women that reproduction is a responsibility closely as-

---

76. Schreiter, *New Catholicity*, 11.

sociated with gender roles. Others still think that certain gender roles are conditioned by biology, while others think that gender roles are mere social construction or artifacts.

If freedom of choice for promoting reproductive health is understood holistically, then autonomy should not neglect the well-being of a child, beginning with the early stage of life, for in the African religion holistic health includes the health of the individual and that of the community in which the individual lives. For most Africans, good health does not only comprise of the physical world, but it is also about the spiritual world. This subject will be deepened by the discussion on African religion and justice later in this study.

Both African feminist ethicists and theologians have to forcibly argue that biotechnology requires bioethics to identify those elements that promote and enhance the holistic life and those that encourage the culture of death and thus must be discarded. African feminists (in collaboration with men) must call for an end to the use of biotechnology that can hamper holistic lives.

2 Justice and Utilitarianism

Utilitarianism takes many forms. This study will focus on a particular form of utilitarianism that has been impacting society for decades: John Stuart Mill's classical utilitarianism. The question that will preoccupy us in this work is what is considered just or unjust according to Mill. Like many other philosophers in the past who have been preoccupied with the question concerning the ultimate principles, John Stuart Mill is not an exception. In fact, Mill wants to establish what really matters in life by developing a moral theory different from his predecessors, whose theories he believes did not go far enough. He insists that a lack of moral standards has most probably made people's beliefs uncertain.[1] He then takes a closer look at other philosophical moral systems' strengths and weaknesses. He concludes that utility is the ultimate principle of morality. Following a summary of Mill's philosophy, I will highlight the connection between utilitarianism and justice.

EXPOSITION OF THE THEORY

Mill defines his theory as the creed that accepts utility as the foundation of morals. Utility, or the greatest principle, holds that "actions are right in proportion, as they tend to promote happiness, wrong, as they tend to produce the reverse of happiness."[2] Mill states that a person's ultimate goal is to live a life of both rich and innumerable pleasures to the fullest extent possible and to avoid pain—these dual goals make up the greatest happiness principle. Utilitarianism is grounded on the assumption that "pleasure and freedom from pain are the only things desirable as ends."[3] Hence, the subject matter of justice in classical utilitarianism is how happiness is maximized for the interest of the general public.

---

1. Mill, *Utilitarianism and On Liberty*, 183.
2. Ibid., 186.
3. Ibid.

Since Mill believes that "human beings have faculties more elevated than the animal appetites,"[4] he argues for the superiority of mental pleasures over bodily ones. It is at this juncture that Mill deviates from Jeremy Bentham, another utilitarian philosopher who lived during the same time as Mill. According to Mill, "it is quite a compatible view with the principle of utility to recognize the fact that some *kinds* of pleasures are more desirable and more valuable than others."[5] This is as a result of judgment made by people who have experienced both kinds of pleasures and that a judgment of such competent judges is considered final.[6]

Mill admits the fact that the theory faces a number of objections. The first objection is that happiness is unattainable and it may mean different things to different people. In response to his critics, Mill writes, "If no happiness is to be had at all by human beings, the attainment of it cannot be the end of morality, or of any rational conduct."[7] He insists that utilitarianism does include not only pursuit of happiness but also that which mitigates unhappiness. However, he also recognizes the fact that such an objection may be genuinely justified, "if by happiness [is] meant a continuity of highly pleasurable excitement."[8] The theory not only speaks of the happiness of all humans but also extends to the "whole sentient creation."[9]

Mill blames "wretched education, and wretched social arrangements," as "the only hindrance to its attainability by all."[10] He then describes happiness as tranquility and excitement, finds its meaning either in private or in public affections. Mill speaks against egoism, and he believes that "selfish interests must be terminated by death: while those who leave after them objects of personal affection and especially those who have cultivated a fellow feeling with the collective interests of mankind, retain as lively an interest in life with on the eve of death as in the vigor of youth and health."[11] With this notion, I do think that Mill seems to link utility with altruism. The concern for others is attributed to good moral

4. Ibid., 187.
5. Ibid.
6. Ibid., 189.
7. Ibid., 190.
8. Ibid., 191.
9. Ibid., 190.
10. Ibid., 191.
11. Ibid.

education. He argues that "genuine private affections, and a sincere interest in the public good, are possible, though in unequal degree, to every rightly brought up human being."[12] Classical utilitarianism asserts that the suffering caused by poverty and diseases can be reduced to minimum limits. It is also asserts that the progress of science holds out a promise for the future in fighting the foes mentioned earlier.[13]

Mill argues that martyrdom does not contradict utility, though there is some denial of happiness for a higher cause. Utilitarian morality does recognize the role of sacrifices not as ends but as means such that "a sacrifice which does not increase, or tend to increase, the sum total of happiness" is wasted.[14] The theory seems not limited or confined to actions of an individual or groups of people and also to those of social institutions. He believes that "laws and social arrangements should place the happiness . . . of every individual as nearly as possible in harmony with the rest of the whole."[15] With respect to one's own happiness and that of others, utilitarianism requires that one be as "strictly impartial as a disinterested and benevolent spectator."[16] To convince his critics, Mill makes use of the Golden Rule of Jesus of Nazareth: "To do as one would be done by, and to love one's neighbor as oneself, constitute the ideal perfection of utilitarian morality."[17] Mill views education and opinion as the means to "establish in the mind of every individual an indissoluble association between his own happiness and the good of the whole."[18]

The second objection Mill faces is related to motives. Mill seems rather skeptical of the role of motives in his theory.[19] Within a utilitarian ethics, whether one acts from duty or from any other motive, the standard of morals depends on the consequence of an action and not on motive. If the standard solely depended on motive, then the standard of morals would shift from focusing on the consequences of acts to that of moral agency and the agent's motive for acting. And if this were the case, then the act would lose its current moral justification.

12. Ibid., 192.
13. Ibid.
14. Ibid., 193.
15. Ibid., 194.
16. Ibid.
17. Ibid.
18. Ibid.
19. Ibid., 195.

The third objection is related to psychology. Mill claims that some critics have raised the issue with utilitarianism that personal qualities, dispositions, emotions, or feelings from which those actions emanate have not been considered by utilitarianism. As a response to the objection, Mill insists that he does not object to the application of psychology to utilitarianism; he insists that there is nothing inconsistent with the theory if people would consider personal qualities or virtues in their moral deliberations. After all, "no known ethical standard decides an action to be good or bad because it is done by a good or bad man."[20] Despite all the criticisms, Mill maintains that "in the long run the best proof of a good character is good actions," and he "resolutely refuse[s] to consider any mental dispositions as good, of which the predominant tendency is to produce bad habit."[21] Mill admits that such a conviction of his critics has made the theory unpopular.

The fourth objection is related to religion. Mill refutes the allegations that utilitarianism is an ungodly doctrine. In response to the allegations, he writes, "If it be a true belief that God desires, above all things, the happiness of his creatures, and that this was his purpose in their creation, utility is not only not a godless doctrine, but more profoundly religious than any other."[22]

The fifth objection is related to moral subjectivism: that utility is an immoral doctrine because a person will ultimately act out of self-interest (expediency), in contrast to acting for the principle of utility. Mill does not rule out the possibility of telling a lie either for the expediency of self or of others, for exceptions are acknowledged by all moralists.[23] While exceptions may be permissible, there is a need to define the limits of what is permissible, and "if the principle of utility is good for anything, it must be good for weighing conflicting utilities against one another and marking out the region within which one or the other preponderates."[24]

The sixth objection is related to the time-factor issue in moral judgment, namely, that there is not enough time for "calculating and weighing

20. Ibid., 196.
21. Ibid., 197.
22. Ibid., 198.
23. Ibid., 199.
24. Ibid.

the effects of any line of conduct on the general happiness" before acting.[25] As a response to this objection, Mill believes that people should make recourse to experience and to "positive beliefs as to the effects of some actions on their happiness; and the beliefs which have thus come down are the rules of morality for the multitude."[26] Mill consolidates his position by considering human foresight as a human quality in any moral deliberation.[27] He concludes by saying that it would be absurd if we did not draw general conclusions from accumulated human experiences.[28] The notion of accumulated experiences as a standard of judgment of moral actions perhaps ranks Mill as a rule utilitarian.

The seventh objection is related to moral exceptions: some people are said to have made exceptions to the breaking of a rule as an excuse in the name of utility holders. Mill's response is that perhaps this is due to the complicated nature of humans, which affects not only utility but also other creeds. It is understandable that accommodation to peculiarities of circumstances is not uncommon, although there is a danger that self-deception and dishonest casuistry could get in. It is only in cases of conflict between secondary principles that primary principles could apply.[29]

Mill dismisses both external and internal factors as insufficient grounds for ultimate moral obligation. He does not in any way deny their contributions in the field of utility. In fact, as regards internal factors, the feeling of a sense of duty as a matter of conscience and all that associated with it (love, sympathy, fear, customs, and experiences) may point to the idea of moral obligation. In fact, even conscience seems to play no crucial role in his theory. Mill claims that this kind of moral obligation derives its force from a "supposed mysterious law" based on a "mass of feeling which must be broken through in order to do what violates our standard of right."[30] Therefore, Mill maintains that internal factors provide a shaky ground for utility. On the other hand, he is still convinced that utility, though a subjective feeling in our own minds, provides the ultimate sanc-

---

25. Ibid., 199.
26. Ibid., 200.
27. Ibid., 201.
28. Ibid.
29. Ibid., 202.
30. Ibid., 205.

tion for morality provided that such a feeling is associated with "conscientious feeling of mankind."[31]

The eighth objection was raised against intuitive morality and whether intuition provides any ground for utility at all. Mill sees no conflict between intuitive morality and utility provided that such a feeling takes into consideration pleasures and pain of others. Also the question of religion seems to not be contradictory to utility since "God does desire above all things the happiness of his creatures."[32] The issue about the relationship between utility and religion was also discussed. Mill thinks that the question of religion seems not contradictory to utility since "God does desire above all things the happiness of his creatures." For Mill, religion would only be justified provided that it provided efficacy to the internal sanctions.[33]

Then, Mill steps up further by introducing the concept of the social nature of humankind as the basis for equality (with an exception for the slave and master relationship and for absolute monarchy) and that only a mutual web of association and cooperation would advance growth, civilization, and the interests of others.[34] He makes his case for utility by appealing to the state of nature as a moral justification. His anthropocentric conception of utility seems to justify his notion of ultimate moral standards. He claims that the state of nature is natural and habitual, so much so that it becomes an inseparable part of every human person. He concludes by saying that religion, law, education, social institutions, opinions, feelings, and others may be important in morality provided that they serve utility as the ultimate moral obligation.

In a further defense of the theory, Mill makes some attempt to lay proofs by appealing to psychology. But before doing that, he starts by saying that utility requires no proof because "questions of ultimate ends do not admit of proof."[35] Utility must be "desired for itself . . . with the utmost intensity."[36] Then he finally turns to psychology to provide a proof that "general happiness is desirable" because "each person desires his

31. Ibid.
32. Ibid., 198.
33. Ibid., 206.
34. Ibid., 207.
35. Ibid., 210.
36. Ibid., 211.

own happiness."[37] Mill notes, "Since each person is a good to that person therefore that of the general happiness is a good to the aggregate of all persons."[38]

Virtue ethics could be accepted if and only if it is part of people's happiness. In Mill's view, utilitarianism is so highly ranked in morality that all other systems of morality have to be judged within the principle of utility. Therefore, Mill considers virtue as means to that ultimate end. He also describes happiness not as "an abstract idea, but a concrete whole . . . virtue being part of it."[39] The concept of the "concrete whole" fits in neatly within Mill's idea that happiness consists not only of physical pleasure but also of nonphysical pleasure, the latter being ranked higher than the former. By such a notion, Mill wants us to believe that a human person is a composite being.

Mill takes the constitution of human nature as a point of departure, namely, that human beings desire nothing else in life apart from happiness as the sole end of human action. He believes that any moral standard must be tested by this criterion. This notion goes back to the definition of utilitarianism earlier mentioned. He claims that such a notion is a proof of fact, evidence, and experience supported by sources of "self-consciousness, and self-observation, and assisted by observation of others."[40] Here he makes a very strong appeal to induction rather than deduction. Social science theory seems to be at play here in the justification of his theory. Since maximization of happiness and minimization of pain is at the very heart of the principle of utility, Mill believes that to desire something other than pleasure or happiness is a "physical and metaphysical impossibility."[41] This is another strong argument of proof for the utility principle.

The consequence of moral actions is the essence of utilitarianism. Performing certain actions in the interest of all people and promoting their happiness is the very soul and essence of the utilitarian moral ideal. The manner in which happiness is properly satisfied in society will be at the center of discussion here. Mill states:

37. Ibid., 210.
38. Ibid.
39. Ibid., 211.
40. Ibid., 213.
41. Ibid., 214.

The idea of justice supposes two things; a rule of conduct, and a sentiment which sanctions the rule. The first must be supposed common to all mankind, and intended for their good. The other (the sentiment) is a desire that punishment may be suffered by those who infringe the rule. There is involved, in addition, the conception of some definite person who suffers by the infringement; whose rights (to use the expression appropriated to the case) are violated by it. And the sentiment of justice appears to me to be, the animal desire to repel or retaliate a hurt or damage to oneself, or to those with whom one sympathizes, widened so as to include all persons, by the human capacity of enlarged sympathy and the human conception of intelligent self-interest. From the latter elements, the feeling derives its morality; from the former, its peculiar impressiveness and energy of self-assertion.[42]

There is an intimate connection between law, moral rights, and justice. Moral rights are those rights that one ought to have. Legal laws may confer rights to someone who ought not to have them or take away or deny rights one who ought to have. In such a case, the person has been unethically and morally entitled or denied these rights. Therefore, such a law is bad and therefore unjust.[43] Justice is done when a person enjoys a right or a good or undergoes an evil when he or she deserves it and injustice occurs when the reverse takes place.[44] Justice ought to be impartial, and preference or favor should be avoided when necessary.[45] Justice calls for equality. However, justice should not be applied arbitrarily:

> Those who think that utility requires distinction of rank, do not consider it unjust that riches and social privileges should be unequally dispensed; but those who think this inequality inexpedient, think it unjust also.[46]

Justice generates moral claims, duties, and obligations. Not all forms of justice generate equal moral duties. Justice calls for perfect moral obligations insofar as justice and rights are correlative. Mill concludes by saying:

---

42. Ibid., 225.
43. Ibid., 218.
44. Ibid.
45. Ibid., 219.
46. Ibid., 220.

> Justice implies something which it is not only right to do, and wrong not to do, but which some individual person can claim from us as his moral right. No one has a moral right to our generosity or beneficence, because we are not morally bound to practice those virtues towards any given individual.[47]

Critique

Mill's utility is anthropocentric and altruistic in nature, and the theory tends to promote the happiness of all people with impartiality. Utility encompasses not only individual humans but also other sentient creation.[48] This notion implies that sociopolitical and economic institutions have to take into account decisions or actions that may have a serious impact on other people's lives and other creatures. Mill considers utility to include not only bodily pleasure but also nonbodily pleasure.[49] He also suggests that human experiences and observations play a very important part in moral deliberations.[50]

Despite utilitarianism's positive points, there are, however, some dark sides. First, the moral and social value of the human person is determined by the way his or her actions produce or contribute to the overall happiness or satisfaction of all. In other words, actions are right if they produce the overall happiness or mitigate pain, and actions are wrong if they produce pain. The difficulty with this ethical theory is that it is unclear how overall happiness ought to trickle down to each individual person and, thus, it becomes a justice issue.

Second, utility is a kind of *ethical consequentialism* that ignores the fact that humans at times are incapable of foreseeing the long-term effects of their actions in every moment of moral deliberation. It's hard to determine actions every moment that would most likely produce the greatest happiness or mitigate happiness.

Third, utility leads to *naturalistic fallacy*; Mill believes that humanity desires nothing else but pleasure. And since one desires one's own happiness, Mill then concludes that one would necessarily desire happiness of

---

47. Ibid., 223
48. Ibid., 190.
49. Ibid., 186.
50. Ibid., 187.

others. This argument infers *ought* from *is*. Morality is about much more than simply desires.

Fourth, utility leads to a *philosophical reductionism* in the sense that if any theory would have to stand any credibility, it should be reduced to utility, and if not it must be rejected. I think this is a philosophical oversimplification; concepts about God or religion, for example, are more complex than what Mill might have conceived.

Fifth, Mill's description of happiness as absence of pain or as the experience of excitement or tranquility seems not to capture the real meaning of happiness for most people.

Six, utility does not address the root cause of evil and suffering in the world, and it is possible that wretched education and wretched social arrangements may simply be symptoms of a deeper problem.

3 Justice and Libertarianism

In *Anarchy, State, and Utopia*, Robert Nozick constructs a theory of entitlement founded on the principle that every person has natural rights to life, liberty, and property. His notion of the state is then justified when solely confined to providing security to these rights. He believes that the only reason that the government has a right to coerce its citizens is for the protection and the defense of the state. Nozick maintains that no state can be justified other than the minimal state that he proposes, since a more extensive state inevitably violates individuals' rights. In this section, I will take up the three principles of justice (acquisition of goods, transfer of goods, and rectification of unjust distribution) in general and examine the principles of justice within the realm of free choice and equality of opportunity.

EXPOSITION OF THE THEORY

The subject matter of justice in libertarianism is how individuals are legitimately or rightfully entitled to private property. Also, it is how individuals freely acquire unowned things and freely exchange them with someone else. Drawing on Locke's social contract theory, Nozick's theory of entitlement is based on the principle that every person has absolute rights to life, liberty, and possessions.[1]

In order to fully understand Nozick's entitlement theory, we need to look briefly at his understanding of the minimal state. His discussion is based on two systems of distributive justice. First, the entitlement theory is based on the assumption that "there is no central distribution, no persons or group entitled to control all the resources, jointly deciding how they are to be doled out."[2] Second, the end-state theory, which Nozick opposes, is built on the assumption that there is a central agency for redistribution of goods that makes a more extensive state unattractive. He

---

1. Nozick, *Anarchy, State, and Utopia*, 10.
2. Ibid., 149.

believes that in a free society, whenever a person gets something, "he gets it from others who give to him in exchange for something, or as a gift."[3] Therefore, things come into this world with ownership. Nozick's slogan, "From each as they choose, to each as they are chosen,"[4] seems to sum up his theory.

Nozick maintains that someone owns property through a legitimate means of distribution based on the principles of acquisition and transfer. He believes that it is through this process of distribution that principles of justice in holding are developed. According to Nozick, the process of distribution involves three major steps, or principles: first, the original acquisition of holdings and appropriation of unheld things;[5] second, the transfer of holdings from one person to another;[6] and third, the rectification of injustices in holdings, especially after "some people steal from others, or defraud them, or enslave them, seizing their product and preventing them from living as they choose or forcibly exclude others from competing in exchanges."[7] To summarize, the three principles of just distribution are related, in that "the holdings of a person are just if he is entitled to them by the principles of justice in acquisition and transfer, or by the principle of rectification of injustice."[8]

Nozick also states that the entitlement theory is historical. He claims that his theory is historical because it deals with whatever actually happened in that process of acquisition and transfer.[9] Distribution is just provided that goods distributed or exchanged follow a legitimate process of distribution. He also extends historicity to the principle of rectification of injustices. He states:

> This principle uses historical information about previous situations and injustices done in them (as defined by the first two principles of justice and rights against interference), and the information about the actual course of events that flowed from these injustices,

3. Ibid.
4. Ibid., 160.
5. Ibid., 150.
6. Ibid.
7. Ibid., 152.
8. Ibid., 153.
9. Ibid.

until the present, and it yields a description (or descriptions) of holdings in the society.[10]

While comparing entitlement theory with the end-state theory, Nozick seems convinced that welfare economics is based on end-state principles that are unhistorical on the assumption that the end-state theory lacks information "others consider relevant in assessing a distribution."[11] He strongly defends his theory against other forms of distribution based either on merit, ability, need, or usefulness to society, claiming that "there is no natural dimension or weighed sum or combination of a small number of natural dimensions that yields the distribution generated in accordance with the principle of entitlement."[12] He views his theory of justice as rational and nonarbitrary because the system of transfer of entitlements is not spinning its gears aimlessly; thus, he adds, "people have reasons and aims why so."[13] Nozick concludes his argument by saying that since entitlement theory defends "individual aims of individual transactions," he does not see the need "for patterned principles in capitalist society."[14] Since patterned principles, such as distribution based on merit or need, require end-state theory, an extensive state other than a minimal state would arise, and it would violate individual rights. It is apparent that Michael Walzer's slogan, "To each according to one's needs, and from each according to one's ability"[15] seems to upset Nozick's entitlement theory. For Nozick, production of goods and distribution are inseparable, and "things come into the world already attached to people having entitlement over them."[16]

Nozick rejects recipient-oriented distributive principles of justice that ignore the rights of givers and transferers. He does not advocate a minimal state in order to provide principles of redistribution of primary goods to everyone in the society, but simply to protect individual rights. He argues that any state more extensive than this would violate these rights.

10. Ibid., 152.
11. Ibid., 155.
12. Ibid., 157.
13. Ibid., 159.
14. Ibid.
15. Walzer, *Spheres of Justice*, 25.
16. Nozick, *Anarchy, State, and Utopia*, 160.

Freedom of Choice in Free Exchange

Nozick maintains that exchanges are voluntary.[17] The question that can be asked is, what is the level of freedom that may be required in the so-called free exchange or transaction? Nozick challenges those who believe that exchange between persons may be involuntary because of the notion that one person may face severely limited options:

> Whether a person's actions are voluntary depends on what it is that limits his alternatives. If facts of nature do so, the actions are voluntary. Other people's actions place limits on one's available opportunities. Whether this makes ones' resulting action non-voluntary depends upon whether these others had the right to act as they did.[18]

For Nozick, free transaction requires rights of engagement in the parties concerned assuming that they have the moral capabilities needed for a free exchange of goods or services. The entitlement theory assumes that one chooses whomever one wants to engage in a transaction. A person has the right to engage in free transaction with anyone who has the right of engagement.[19] He concludes by saying that "rights to engage in relationships or transactions have hooks on them, which must attach to the corresponding hook of another's right that comes out to meet theirs."[20]

Equality of Opportunity in Free Exchange

Entitlement theory does not take into consideration equality of opportunity in free exchange. Nozick believes that if equality of opportunity were considered, it would worsen the situations of those more favored with opportunity by improving the situation of those less well favored.[21] This consideration would require resources from those who hold them justly, and this situation would infringe upon or violate individual rights.[22] However, Nozick argues:

---

17. Ibid., 262.
18. Ibid.
19. Ibid., 264. Children or those with mental disability do not have the right of engagement because they lack the capacity to make free choices.
20. Ibid.
21. Ibid., 235.
22. Ibid.

> Inequalities are inevitable on the basis that one chooses to transfer to someone who satisfies a certain condition (for example, who can provide him with a certain good or service in exchange, who can do a certain job, who can pay a certain salary) and he would be equally willing to transfer to anyone else who satisfies that condition.[23]

In this discussion, Nozick demonstrates that goods are created and that people have entitlement over them through the principles of justice in acquisition, transfer, and rectification of injustices. I have examined in particular the principle of justice in transfer within the context of freedom of choice and equality of opportunity in free exchange. Regarding these points, Nozick is of the view that limitations of opportunity do not necessarily render contracts or exchanges involuntary and that equality of opportunity would violate individual rights. He argues that production and distribution are inseparable. Therefore, in Nozick's view, an extensive state would violate individual rights.

Critique

In the preface of *Anarchy, State, and Utopia*, Nozick maintains that his book is a "philosophical exploration of issues . . . which arise and interconnect when we consider individual rights and the state."[24] On the one hand, he does caution us that his book does not present a theory of individual right or a precise statement of the principles of the tripartite theory of distributive justice.[25] On the other hand, he claims that his theory rests on some general features such theories would have, if they were implemented.[26] I am of the view that a theory like his, which touches on the very fundamental principle of free exchange, seems to bear a considerable moral impact on wages in the contemporary society.

The question that I hope to deal with here is analytical: that is, to determine whether Nozick's notion of justice in transfer is at all just as he claims to be. One may legitimately ask, what the kind of standard or criterion will determine whether Nozick's principle of justice in transfer is just or otherwise? As will be shown in this discussion, the question of

23. Ibid., 236.
24. Ibid., xii.
25. Ibid.
26. Ibid., xiv.

a just wage is an issue that no one can compare with, not even with that of Wilt Chamberlain's case of having a large income supported by people who would voluntarily buy tickets to watch him play baseball.[27] To proceed with the task of critiquing Nozick's principle of justice in transfer, I wish to set up a point of departure. By way of proceeding, I will employ an internal critique that examines Nozick's historical method in the context of labor and wages.

The Historical Method and Natural Rights

First of all, Nozick is one of the few theorists who manages to keep his readers focused on the importance of individual liberty in free exchange. Nozick, however, is very critical of John Rawls's method of the original position on the assumption that it lacks historicity.[28] While Iris Marion Young, on the one hand, is critical of Nozick's theory of an individualistic model of rights,[29] Susan Moller Okin, on the other hand, makes a different criticism against Nozick: his theory leads to certain absurd conclusions when labor is applied to human reproduction (ownership is a result of labor mixed with things). In her example, because having children involves women's labor, then children can be owned and freely exchanged as private property. Okin believes that this theory may lead to very problematic moral dilemma of matriarchy, slavery, and dystopia.[30]

I will now examine the method underlying Nozick's principle of justice in transfer and see the kind of conclusions that may be reached. First of all, let me ask why he calls his method historical and why its principles just. Can I say that exchange of labor for wages is just simply because the process has been legitimately followed? Nozick calls the principle of justice in transfer just because the actual process of distribution can be traced. For Nozick, justice seems to be a matter of logic. He draws a parallel between truth-preserving and justice-preserving transformations.[31] He makes a contrast with current time-slice principles of distribution that depend on certain patterns. He claims that end-result or end-state principles consider only the results or the matrices of a distribution and

27. Ibid., 161.
28. Ibid., 202.
29. Young, *Politics of Difference*, 55.
30. Okin, *Justice, Gender, and the Family*, 79–87.
31. Nozick, *Anarchy, State and Utopia*, 151.

not the way in which those results come about.³² He also claims that the entitlement theory is not patterned, that is, the distribution neither depends on some merit, need, nor on natural endowment. At this point, Nozick's theory offers a great variety examples of goods generated and how individuals are entitled to them, either from gambling, gift-giving, interests on loans, or even returns on investment, and so on.³³ He believes that the entitlement theory takes into consideration real issues and real people involved in the process of free exchange.

For Nozick, history seems to legitimize and justify the norms of morality. This notion generates a number of questions: Does this mean necessarily that something is right because it is historical? Does history give us the principles of morality? Or do facts dictate ethics and morality? Does the *how* amount to the *ought*? Or is *is* identical to *ought*? Nozick assumes that those involved in the process of free exchange are rational adults who know their rights and how they can discharge or satisfy them. On the other hand, he is less concerned about the extent to which exchanges are voluntary when one may be faced with limited options or opportunity.³⁴ In my view, Nozick is more preoccupied with the historicity of the process than with the concrete and historical individuals involved in such contracts. I argue that since his notion of the historical method does not account seriously for concrete historical individuals in a free-market economy (taking into account a web of relationships and personal understanding of the goods exchanged), this is further proof that his method is inconsistent with his assumptions of individual rights; while his method may satisfy the need for a just wage, it does not adequately provide for a living wage. Personally, I view the notion of a living wage as a justice issue, which Nozick's theory seems to have ignored.

My next concern is the minimal state vis-à-vis rectification of injustices and how Nozick's theory could handle employees who have been unfairly treated by government officials who own private businesses. This is an important concern in relation to the rights of employees. The state would need to have a policy in place to deal with such cases, and thus it would first delineate a proper mode of operation for such transactions between the government officials' business owners and their employees.

32. Ibid.,154.
33. Ibid., 157.
34. Ibid., 262.

As I recall, in the reconstruction of the minimal state, however, Nozick displays a high level of skepticism in the sense that he admits that individuals may be unable to administer justice to themselves and to others because of their propensity to partiality, prejudices, selfishness, or even lack of proper balance in executing justice.[35] Nozick also acknowledges the propensity to egoistic motives in the so-called free exchange. How then can he make us believe in the very people who he also distrusts? He even says, "Investors are not altruistic. They act in their personal and not their class interests."[36] More importantly, it is worth noting that the lack of sufficient knowledge about the values of goods in free market economy is also another factor that can contribute to injustices in Nozick's minimal state.

In the face of all these factors just mentioned, I doubt whether free exchange solely left to personal arrangement between contracting parties could be justly conducted. Some form of regulation may be necessary to maintain checks and balances in a free-market economy. Again, if one assumes that some government officials are also involved in the enterprises of free exchange, how impartial can they be when investigating injustices of those involved in fraud? How will employees recover loses from government officials who have immense political influence within the circle of the judicial justice system? Perhaps one solution to such problems is that politicians or civil servants should be prevented from being involved in private enterprises in order to prevent corruption. To Nozick, doing this would violate individual rights.

Nozick also recognizes the fact that "economically well-off persons desire greater political power in a nonminimal state, because they can use this power to give themselves differential benefits."[37] His view about this problem is that political and economic powers constitute two separate spheres. Since corruption often manifests itself as an illegitimate use of state power for an individual's economic interest, Nozick thinks that doing away with certain uses of political power would drastically reduce its abuse. He believes that the minimal state could accomplish this.[38] In theory, Nozick seems to have only addressed the way to reduce the abuse

---

35. Ibid., 11.
36. Ibid., 253.
37. Ibid., 272.
38. Ibid.

of power in the minimal state but not how to address injustices perpetrated by government officials in a free-market economy because of their complacency in prosecuting each other. Perhaps the only solution to end the cycle of injustices would be to bar government officials from engaging in private businesses. According to Nozick, however, this measure would necessarily violate liberty rights.

From the illustration above, it seems that Nozick does not offer a clear criterion by which to counterpoise injustices within the minimal state. His theory does not go far enough to resolve the conflict of rights in the minimal state. Based on this assumption, I would argue that if this conflict remains unresolved, it would jeopardize the course of justice for employees in the free market economy. This may also be an indication that, in reality, his minimal state is unable to protect individual rights to a living wage when deduced from his assumption of rights. Therefore, I argue that employees would be vulnerable to injustices in Nozick's minimal state.

The internal critique that I have attempted to make on Nozick's theory of justice reveals some important points: First, libertarianism is a political theory that places the individual rights of life, liberty, and property at the center of the moral discourse. Second, this theory seeks to justify the creation of the minimal state. Third, the conclusions derived from Nozick's basic assumption of the natural rights are seemingly inconsistent with his historical method on the basis that a just wage as a living wage derives directly from such an assumption. Therefore, I argue that Nozick's anthropological assumptions of rights have to be consistent with his method. I argue that since public regulatory policy is required to ensure that contracts or free exchanges in the private sector take into account the interests of both parties (employees and employers), this move may require more than just the minimal state Nozick proposes.

4 Justice and Communitarianism

In *Spheres of Justice: A Defense of Equality and Pluralism*, Michael Walzer is considered by many scholars as a communitarian social contract philosopher. Walzer constructs a theory of justice in defense of equality and pluralism, namely different spheres of justice have different methods of distributing goods.

EXPOSITION OF THE THEORY

The subject matter of justice in communitarianism is how human society distributes social goods:

> Human society is a distributive community. That's not all it is, but it is importantly that: we come together to share, divide, and exchange. We also come together to make the things that are shared, divided, and exchanged; but that very making—work itself—is distributed among us in a division of labor. My place in the economy, my standing in the political order, my reputation among my fellows, my material holdings: all these come to me from other men and women.[1]

The primary principle of distributive justice is that social goods have social meanings: men and women come together for a reason and have to have the knowledge or the idea of the goods they want to create, make, divide, or share with others.[2] The distributive criteria and arrangements are intrinsic not to the goods themselves but to the conception and the production of goods by people at the end of the assembly line; the social meanings given to goods entails that justice is also a social construction.[3] The value of goods is dependent on society, which determines their move-

---

1. Walzer, Spheres of Justice, 3.
2. Ibid., 6. Note the term *distribute* according to Walzer connotes *allocate*, *share*, *divide*, or *exchange*.
3. Ibid., 8–9.

ments: to whom and for what reasons. Consequently there is no universal value of goods.[4]

There are two kinds of principles that govern distribution. First, there is the internal principle of distributive justice that arises from internal decisions of members who have similar shared understanding of the social goods. Second, there is the external principle of distributive justice that arises when members extend social goods to strangers. The latter principle will be discussed later in this section.

Given that membership in a political community is the primary subject matter of distributive justice and that goods have social meanings, it is fair to say that Michael Walzer's method of justice is historical: it is a social contract made by real and concrete people in political communities with various customs, norms, traditions, and cultures.

When do we have a just society? Or when are distributions of goods just or unjust? Walzer, unlike Rawls or Nozick, offers a different theory of justice, which not only encompasses an identity of distribution (similar goods with a similar distribution, known as simple equality). Rather, it is about differences (inequalities within the boundary of the same sphere of distribution) and similarities (equality that admits a variety of goods held in the same sphere): different goods with a different method of distributions in different spheres, and different goods with different meanings with different ways of distribution. This is called *complex equality* as opposed to *simple equality*:

> Simple Equality is simple distributive conditions, so that if I have fourteen hats and you have fourteen hats, we are equal. And it is all to the good if hats are dominant, for then our equality is extended through all the spheres of life. On the view that I shall take here, however, we simply have the same number of hats, and it is unlikely that hats will be dominant for long. Equality is a complex relation of persons, mediated by the goods we make, share, and divide among ourselves; it is not an identity of possessions. It requires then, a diversity of distributive criteria that mirrors the diversity of social goods.[5]

Justice admits inequalities provided they are exercised or confined within the same sphere of distribution and that the conversion of one good into another follows the principle of inner logic that is intrinsic to

---

4. Ibid., 7.
5. Ibid., 18.

the goods in question.⁶ The opposite of this logic is domination and tyranny. This means that invading another sphere or crossing into another territory illegally is injustice. In restoring justice in a political community, Walzer justifies the use of complex equality in his own terms to fight against domination and tyranny:

> The regime of complex equality is the opposite of tyranny. It establishes a set of relationships such that domination is impossible. In formal terms, complex equality means that no citizen's standing in one sphere or with regard to one social good can be undercut by his standing in some other sphere, with regard to some other good. Thus, citizen X may be chosen over citizen Y for political office, and then the two of them will be unequal in the sphere of politics. But they will not be unequal generally so long as X's office gives him no advantages over Y in any other sphere.... So long as office is not a dominant good, is not generally convertible, office holders will stand, or at least can stand, in a relation of equality to the men and women they govern.⁷

Distribution, in Walzerian terms, means *allocate, divide, share*, or *exchange*. What are the principles by which social goods can be distributed justly to members or strangers? Why does someone share or exchange a certain kind of good and not necessarily another? What is the method behind these principles? Is it a mere convention or social arrangements? Walzer comes up with three distributive criteria that "meet the requirements of the open-handed principle": the principles of free exchange, desert, and need.⁸ First, in the free exchange principle, money is the medium of exchange, and yet the goods being exchanged should reflect their social meanings:

> In theory at least, free exchange creates a market within which all goods are convertible into other goods through the medium of money. There are no dominant goods and no monopolies. Hence the successive divisions that obtain will directly reflect the social meanings of the goods that are divided. For each bargain, trade, sale, and purchase will have been agreed to voluntarily by men

---

6. Ibid., 19.

7. Ibid., 19–20.

8. Ibid., 21. By "open-ended principle," Walzer means that the exact outcomes in the distribution are not always predictable.

and women who know what the meaning is, who are indeed its makers. Every exchange is a revelation of social meaning.[9]

How free are these exchanges? Should there be a set of boundaries? Do people set limits within a pluralist market? The principle of complex equality ensures that boundaries or limits are in place to protect the distributions of goods in spheres:

> For money seeps through across all boundaries—this is the primary form of illegal immigration; and just where one ought to try to stop it is a question of expediency as well as of principle. Failure to stop it at some reasonable point has consequences throughout the range of distributions.[10]

Let us examine these templates and see the results. Some person called Y having the social good X because Y has the social good A must be justified by establishing the social meanings of these two goods: the intrinsic connection between A and X. If the connection between A and X is unfounded, given that A and X have distinctive social meanings, and they belong to different spheres of distribution, then there is an invasion of sphere A upon sphere X causing an illegitimate crossing, which leads to domination and tyranny. Employing the principle of complex equality (respecting different distributing principles in different spheres) in distributing social goods in various spheres of distributions regulates the process of distribution and thus stops, contains, or controls monopoly, domination, and tyranny.

Can one predict the exact outcome of distribution in free exchange? Walzer notes:

> Free exchange is obviously open-ended; it guarantees no particular distributive outcome. . . . The market is radically pluralistic in its operations and its outcomes, infinitely sensitive to the meanings that individuals attach to goods.[11]

Second, the principle of desert seems even more complicated and pluralistic than the principle of free exchange when applied to the principle of complex equality: "No x would ever be distributed without regard to its social meaning; for, without attention to what x is, it is conceptu-

---

9. Ibid.
10. Ibid., 22.
11. Ibid., 21.

ally impossible to say that x is deserved."[12] It seems difficult for some to determine how to distribute love, influence, or politics to others through the principle of desert or merit. How one can establish that a person deserves to be loved, elected, or employed? How is love, politics, or public office distributed? To answer these questions one would be required to deal with this other question: what's the inner logic or intrinsic connection between the person or persons and these goods called *love*, *office*, or *political power*? For Y to deserve X there should be an inner logic between the person, Y, and the social good, X: "Desert seems to require an especially close connection between particular social goods and particular persons, whereas justice only sometimes requires a connection of some sort."[13] Failure to establish this connection leads to monopoly, domination, and tyranny. The lack of this sort of connection in political governance produces totalitarians and tyrants. The principle of complex equality controls or eliminates domination and tyranny in the distribution of social goods.[14]

Desert and need are different spheres, and thus they operate differently. For example, Y needs food, but Y does not necessarily deserve it. Need and desert are not one and the same thing. "Desert does not have the urgency of need and it does not involve having (owning and consuming) in the same way."[15]

Third, the principle of need takes the form of the Marxian principle of distribution: "From each according to his ability, to each according to his needs." The trouble with this principle of need could be that its application may be limited. How will one distribute power, jobs, love, influence, and so on? Will it be according to needs or ability? Are these, strictly speaking, needs? Whose needs: employees or employers? Can needs and desert overlap? The principle of need forms its own sphere of distribution, and thus it must be respected as such.[16] The criterion of complex equality applies here, though in a different way, without altering the inner logic of distribution. This time around, the preoccupation about the principle of need as opposed to the principle of merit is not about the connection

12. Ibid., 23.
13. Ibid., 24.
14. Ibid., 19, 28.
15. Ibid.
16. Ibid., 26.

between Y and X; rather it is about the lack of this connection: "Needed goods distributed to needy people in proportion to their neediness are obviously not dominated by any other goods. It's not having y, but only lacking x that is relevant."[17]

Lacking X leads to lacking Y because having Y requires having X legitimately. Having Y because of having X without understanding the social meaning of X, without establishing the inner logic between the social goods X and Y in relation to the social understanding of these goods, is domination and tyranny and therefore unjust. It is injustice if one lacks X. However, lacking Y is not necessarily injustice; having Y because of X without an internal connection between the two is necessarily injustice.

Membership in a political community is the primary social good upon which the distribution of other social goods totally depends. To access these goods one must be a member, one who understands the social meanings of such goods: one who knows how the goods to be shared, divided, or exchanged came into existence. How can nonmembers or strangers within the common frontiers or borders enjoy these social goods? Membership cannot be shared among its members because it is already theirs.[18] Membership has to be shared with strangers through "the external principle of mutual aid."[19] Failure to admit strangers—for example, failure to include refugees into our political community and to share membership with them—leads to inequality, domination, and tyranny. Admitting strangers into a particular political community is a political decision undertaken by government's policy makers regarding immigration, naturalization, and citizenship.[20]

What's the inner philosophical justification or the ethical and moral basis of this admission? Is distributing membership to strangers like refugees and other immigrants an act of charity, philanthropy, or justice? What's the moral force of duties towards strangers? In this regard, Walzer admits the fact that a clear philosophical reason for the principle of mutual aid is not easy to come by. And the lack of such a justifying principle might the render justice a nonmoral obligation:

17. Ibid.
18. Ibid., 32.
19. Ibid., 33.
20. Ibid., 34.

> The philosophical grounds of the principle are hard to specify. . . . The force of the principle is uncertain, in part because of its own vagueness, in part because it sometimes comes up against the internal force of social meanings. And these meanings can be specified, and are specified, through the decision-making processes of the political community.[21]

The lack of a solid philosophical justification of admitting strangers into a political community means that "justice would be nothing more than non-coercion, good faith, and good Samaritanism—a matter entirely of external principle."[22] What is an external principle? It is a principle that calls for the distribution of certain goods to strangers who lack the social meanings of such goods being distributed. Because such distribution is not based on the principle of inner logic, the process entails a non–morally binding obligation. Walzer thinks that love of neighbor as it is illustrated in the parable of the good Samaritan is non–morally binding, and it does not command and demand a morally binding response. Rather, it is a philanthropic venture left to one's liberty and initiative, and therefore it remains optional. This kind of thinking reflects the Nozickian philanthropic charity.

Critique

Walzer, while dealing with the principles of justice, pays close attention to the uniqueness of political communities that enact the principles of justice. He claims that his method is inductive and historical: it is a social contract, which deals with reality: real people and real issues. In so doing, he comes up with the principles that reflect the uniqueness of each community and the method of distributing social goods to its members who have a shared understanding of such goods—pluralism. Human experience is the centerpiece of his social theory of justice.

At other times, Walzer discusses cases or examples, and he seems not to draw any conclusions or principles from them. Walzer argues that justice is not only a matter of distribution; rather it is a matter of understanding the meaning of distributions and social meanings of goods. He also admits that the outcomes of distributions, being pluralistic in nature, are not easy to predict due to factors that come into play, for example,

21. Ibid., 33, 43.
22. Ibid.

how free markets can alter or affect distributions. Based on these and other factors, Walzer argues that the principles of justice—free exchange, desert, and need—are open ended, leaving room for more possibilities. Life is a complex reality in which the relationships of persons are mediated by social goods. Rather than believing that life is simple, he proposes that the regime of complex equality fits better in this equation.

Walzer's effort is not directed towards eliminating inequalities. Otherwise, in so doing, one eliminates complexities and pluralism and welcomes simple equality. Rather, Walzer justifies inequalities provided they are confined within their spheres of distributions. Justice means respecting different spheres with different distributing principles of social goods. The regime of complex equality establishes the right relationships in the spheres of distributions to eliminate monopoly, domination, and tyranny.

Walzer also admits the fact that principles internal to social goods are insufficient in dealing with the whole range of justice. Walzer employs the external principle of justice in dealing with distributing social goods to strangers: the principle of mutual aid. Walzer, however, fails to provide the principle of mutual aid with a solid morally binding basis. In his understanding, justice as charity means that justice does not generate moral obligations, and therefore it is a non-morally binding principle, in contrast to the way charity is depicted in Christianity in the parable of the good Samaritan. Doing charity is the work of those who choose to do so voluntarily or out of their free choice as philanthropists. Because social goods such as membership cannot be extended to nonmembers due to their lack of the social meaning of such a good, strangers such as refugees and other immigrants are left to the care of philanthropists and the legislation of politicians, who either admit or reject them under the law of the land. Walzer provides some internal criteria, which protects a limited group of strangers; birth, kinship, political, and social affiliations can justify the distribution of membership to strangers. How about those who will not fall under these categories? What is a justifying principle of justice in such a case? Walzer acknowledges that it is difficult to come up with a philosophical basis of the mutual aid principle.

Does Walzer's method provide the principles of justice because it is historical? Is history equal to ethical principles? Do facts of history tell us how to be just? Is *is* the same as *ought*? This is what Walzer's method seems to suggest. Walzer seems to claim that goods in and of themselves do not have an intrinsic value and that their value depends upon the community's understanding of such goods by conception and production. Furthermore, Walzer's defense of equality and pluralism seems to suggest that there are no principles that hold true for all times, people, and places. Human experience, the major component of Walzer's method, shows that we can never get it right but closer to it. No person has the capacity to know something a hundred percent. Human experience adds something new to the growth of human knowledge. Walzer seems to suggest that the existence of universal principles of justice is inconceivable given that human experience is at the core of his theory and that human experience differs from community to community and from place to place. Does it mean that Walzer is an ethical relativist? Is this not a simplistic conclusion about his theory?

Conclusion to Part 1

Every theory of justice discussed in part 1 was an attempt to deal with the distribution of justice in society. The ideas of justice are diverse, as are the ways of administering it, as seen with feminism, liberalism, libertarianism, utilitarianism, and communitarianism. There have been some strengths and limitations in each of these theories, rendering them inadequate to fully address the ethical and moral problems of our contemporary world: degrading inequalities, injustices, monopoly, domination, oppression, and tyranny. Failure in resolving these ethical and moral problems threatens the survival of individuals, communities, and, indeed, the whole world. Furthermore, in these theories, the solid basis for administering justice is lacking or weak. These lacunae need to be filled. Part 2 attempts to seek a new understanding of justice from the biblical and African perspectives of justice.

PART 2

Possible Sources for Constructing a Macrotheory of Justice

The critique of philosophical theories of justice suggests that an alternative theory is critical to a better understanding of justice. This time our attention turns to Africa. What can the continent of Africa contribute to justice issues? Some parts of the continent are suffering from past and current injustices, due to the internal and external factors: tribalism, ethnocentrism, slavery, colonialism and neocolonialism, racism, sexism, religious discrimination and persecution, political dictatorship, corruption, post–cold war conflicts, geopolitical interests or realpolitik, and so on. In *Basic Human Rights and the Humanitarian Crises in Sub-Saharan Africa: Ethical Reflections*, I examined the nature and scope of the humanitarian crises, which led to the influx of refugees and internally displaced persons (IDPs) in sub-Saharan Africa. In such crises, these groups of people, particularly women and children, had been deprived of their basic rights to security, subsistence, and liberty. The 1994 Rwandan genocide, which claimed the deaths of almost a million Tutsis and moderate Hutus, demonstrates such injustices.[1] People across the world have wondered about what went wrong with Rwanda, a country with a Christian majority and

---

1. See Msoka, *Humanitarian Crises in Sub-Saharan Africa*, 1–26.

with rich moral traditions aimed at protecting human life and property. Certainly, something terribly went wrong between Hutus and Tutsis, who speak one language and share common customs and traditions.

Based on the worst scenario posed by the crises, the need for rediscovering, reviving, restoring, and reclaiming the cultural moral traditions of respect for human life and property is timely, imperative, and critical to restoring justice and peace in sub-Saharan Africa. The task now is to identify African cultural narratives of justice, which can be described as *cosmotheandrism* (the interrelation of the nature, God, and humans), or, as the term is known in Kichagga and Kiswahili, *ORUM* and *UMUMTU*. What does African cultural narrative look like? How can these narratives offer new insights to the theory of justice in ways different from liberalism, libertarianism, and so on? If these cultural narratives depict the African social milieu, the question becomes: are the narratives going to offer an intellectual appeal to liberals, libertarians, or feminists? What kind of the principles of justice can be retrieved from such narratives?

5 African Cultural Narratives of Justice

NATURE AND SCOPE OF AFRICAN NARRATIVES OF JUSTICE

The term, cosmotheandrism, is derived from a combination of three Greek words: *cosmos* (world), *theos* (God), and *anthropos* (man).[1] Cosmotheandrism is synonymous with African narratives known as ORUM (oruka, rua, mdu) or UMUMTU (ulimwengu, mungu, mtu).[2] Throughout this book, the terms *cosmotheandrism*, *ORUM*, and *UMUMTU* will be used interchangeably. In so doing, readers across the board will have a wide range of choice of language.

The African moral universe focuses on God, nature, and humankind and how they are interrelated or how they interact with each other. In African religion, the cultural narratives of cosmotheandrism, ORUM, or UMUMTU represent a complex view of reality, consisting of multiple threads or webs of relationships intimately connected with each other. The African moral universe is intimately connected to African religion. Hence, ethics, morality, politics, economics, and religion are inseparable, as Laurenti Magesa, a strong proponent of African religion, explains:

> The universe is a composite of divine, spirit, human, animate and inanimate elements, hierarchically perceived, but directly related, and always interacting with each other. Some of these elements are visible, others invisible. They correspond to the visible and invisible spheres of the universe: the visible world being composed

---

1. Msoka, *Basic Human Rights*, 129.

2. In the Chagga dialect spoken in Uru, Moshi District, Kilimanjaro region in Tanzania, Africa, the acronym ORUM connotes the following: *oruka* means "universe," "world," or "nature," *rua* means "God," *mdu* means "humankind." Synonymous to ORUM in the Kiswahili language is UMUMTU: *ulimwengu* means "universe" or "world," *mungu* means "God," and *mtu* means "humankind." The Kiswahili language is spoken in East and Central Africa: Tanzania, Kenya, parts of Uganda, Rwanda, Burundi, Democratic Republic of Congo, and the Comoro Islands. The term *mtu* represents the living and the living dead or ancestors, as well as the unborn.

of creation, including humanity, plants, animals and inanimate beings, and the invisible world being the sphere of God, the ancestors and the spirits.[3]

It is worth examining the nature of the African cultural narratives of cosmotheandrism, ORUM, or UMUMTU. In understanding the African moral universe, God is perhaps the most critical element of the cosmotheandric relationship. According to Magesa, "at the top of the hierarchy of the universe is the Divine Force, which is both the primary and the ultimate life giving Power, Creator, Sustainer, and the Holy."[4] If God is life-sustaining and life-giving power, the community is called upon to be the same: "as God is and does, so human beings must be so."[5]

God, at top of the hierarchy, has a lot to do with the rest of the relationships in cosmotheadrism, ORUM, or UMUMTU. The living dead or the ancestors exercise a unique role upon their descendants because they are the channels of the vital force. These relationships demand fidelity to the moral traditions, which promote abundant life, in such a way that any infidelity is punishable. (This issue about punishment will be tackled at a later stage.) In African religion, it is believed that the ancestors "are the watchdog[s] of the moral behavior of the individual, the family, the clan, and the entire society with which they are associated."[6]

Divine attributes such as life-giver and sustainer of power are believed to have an impact upon the African ethos. Infidelity to the moral traditions of the ancestors may lead to diseases, drought, famine, plagues, and the like. These events can cause social disorder and jeopardize the abundant life. Hence, the subject matter of justice in Africa can be summed up as follows: it is how God, humankind, and nature are interrelated and interact; it is how these relationships are ordered in the universe to produce harmony and peace. Above all, it is how these relationships promote abundant life in the community. Therefore, justice is measured by the way the individuals enjoy abundant life in the community called UMUMTU.

It was said that infidelity to the African moral traditions will summon punishment. Who punishes? Is it God, the ancestors, or the spirits?

---

3. Magesa, *African Religion*, 44.
4. Ibid., 44–45.
5. Ibid., 45.
6. Ibid., 51.

In a way, God is believed to punish evil people by allowing evil things to happen to them and to the community. Nevertheless, the African God does not only punish by allowing bad things to happen to people due to their misconduct, but God is also good, forgiving, and merciful. God, apart from allowing a disruption of social order, is also the restorer of cosmotheandric order. As Magesa says, "God is also Helper in Trouble, Healer, Guardian along the Path, Ruler, Water Giver, Distributor of Goodness, and Sustainer of All."[7]

The belief in the spirit world is perhaps the most complicated notion in understanding the nature of UMUMTU. As complicated as the spirit world may be, and despite being invisible, it cannot easily be ignored or brushed aside because of the immense power of influence it can bear upon the African moral thinking and behavior. Which category in the order of UMUMTU does the spirit world fall under? Is it under nature, God, or humankind? To determine its category, the nature of the spirit world is worth examining.

The spirit world consists of two major kinds of spirits: first, spirits of the living dead, those who were part of human existence, and second, spirits of nonhuman existence—these are spirits that inhabit animals and places like rivers, streams, lakes, oceans, seas, mountains, and so on. Regarding the nature of the spirits of the living dead, Magesa explains that human spirits "are spirits of children who pass away without proper initiation or without children of their own, or spirits of people who upon death, did not receive a proper burial."[8]

Magesa argues that both human and nonhuman spirits can either dwell in the sky above or on the earth. If their domicile can either be on the above or on the earth, what impact do they have upon nature and humankind? First of all, Magesa falls short of distinguishing the type of spirits that predominantly live on the earth and those that live above. Lack of this distinction leaves one to wonder which spirits cause harm and which bring about good fortune to the people. However, one idea seems clear to Magesa, namely, that the "spirits of the below are generally considered weaker than the spirits of the above."[9] To beg the question: are

---

7. Ibid., 49.
8. Ibid., 56.
9. Ibid.

they human or nonhuman spirits, since both of these can either inhabit the air or the earth? Are they weaker in causing harm?

Nevertheless, Magesa makes a significant point in associating the spirits of the below with the vital force of the clan system, the totem.[10] As spirits are believed to inhabit animate beings, like animals (crocodile, deer, and so on), whichever clan the totem is associated with these animals, no harm can be caused to the community by these animals. Maintaining the totemic system keeps balance and harmony in UMUMTU, which is regarded as critical to justice and peace in the universe.

Nature (both animate and inanimate beings) is integral to the *community*, UMUMTU. Ecological protection (land, air, water, vegetation, and so on) contributes to abundant life for the present and future generations. This proposition portrays nature as the bearer of justice and dignity. Hence, duties of justice toward nature are sacred in African religion, given the sacred character of UMUMTU. The rediscovery and use of this image can restore dignity to nature.

Another point worth considering is the influence or the impact the human spirits have in the community. As already pointed out, the moral legacy of the living dead, who are still considered a vital part of the African moral universe, UMUMTU, has a lot to do with their descendants and the world at large. The human spirits who once lived an immoral life on earth are the most feared because of the harm they can cause or inflict on people to get attention, recognition, and appeasement.[11] By recognizing and appeasing these spirits, harmony, stability, and order are sustained in the universe. However, some people are gifted with the science and the technology for tapping the spiritual powers either for enhancing life (medicine) or destroying it (witchcraft).[12] Thus, the latter is considered to be the enemy of life and seen as the cause of disharmony and disorder in the universe.

Based on the previous discussion, one can hardly fail to know the direction this discussion is taking so far. Basically, the African religion, an encompassing reality, is critical to promoting deeper justice and peace. Magesa concurs with this interpretation of African religion:

---

10. Ibid., 57.
11. Ibid., 58.
12. Ibid., 59.

> Since it involves the whole of life, whatever one thinks, says, or does is religious or, at least, can have religious implications. At all times in a person's life, a religious consciousness is always explicitly or implicitly present. In no way is anything understood apart from the context of God, the ancestors and the spirits; in no way is any thought, word, or act understood except in terms of good and bad, in the sense that such an attitude or behavior diminishes life.[13]

If the African ethos stresses the fact of interaction among different webs of relationships in UMUMTU (God, humans, and spirits) one wonders who really takes moral responsibility for actions in African religion. Is it God, humans including the ancestors, spirits, or it is a combination of all these? Magesa responds, "The agents for moral action in African religion are the vital forces of the entire created universe [in] both the visible and invisible worlds."[14] One would expect Magesa to demonstrate how God, at the top of the UMUMTU relationship, plays out in the moral agency as a noncreated being. Yes, God plays the greatest role as a life-giver and a sustainer. As God is the giver and sustainer of life, so also are we. This moral imperative is critical to living out the demands of greater justice and peace in the community.

Because African religion considers divinity the essential component of UMUMTU, nature is considered sacred.[15] This proposition calls for sacred duties towards nature. Therefore, manhandling nature is considered unethical and immoral. Since human life is heavily dependent upon nature for its sustenance and survival, protecting our planet's resources and sharing them equitably among peoples is imperative, and thus it is morally binding. As Magesa argues, "in African religious ethical understanding, the earth is given to humanity as a gratuitous gift and all human beings possess an equal claim to it and resources it offers."[16] Hence, any monopoly of the earth's resources by a few is greed and therefore considered unethical and immoral. Are the earth's resources like land and the like owned individually or communally? In African religion, land is not an owned property in the strict sense of the word because it belongs to the clan or tribe, and the ancestors passed it on to their descendants:

---

13. Ibid., 60.
14. Ibid.
15. Ibid., 61.
16. Ibid., 63.

> In African ethical thought, the universe has been lent by God to humanity through the ancestors and the living leaders to use on the condition that it must be kept in good order and used by all for the promotion of life, good relationship and peace, at least within the clan or ethnic group. If these conditions are broken, humanity forfeits the right to it and often deserves chastisement if reparations in the form of sacrifice or offering are not offered.[17]

A proper and adequate understanding of UMUMTU is critical to knowing the nature and scope of the African moral universe. It is within this worldview that the African understanding of ethics and morality and that of social justice in particular can be explored, discussed, or debated. The impact African religion has on how society is organized and shaped is a point of interest in this discussion. In traditional Africa, religion and politics are fused together and hardly inseparable. In the following section, the relationship between politics and religion is discussed.

Administration of Justice

So far, three main systems of political organizations have been identified in traditional black Africa:

1. Kinship, as practiced among the !Kung people of the Kalahari Desert Basin of Botswana and Namibia, is rooted in consanguineous relationship and organized in bands led by headmen.[18] Magesa emphasizes that "the headmen position is hereditary."[19] The nature of authority consists of persuasion and arbitration:

   > Headmen's responsibility can be characterized rather as ontological and moral authority that establishes unity of the group symbolically (headman) and maintains order by force of persuasion and exemplary goodness (leader).[20]

2. Lineage, practiced among the Tallensi of Ghana and Nuer, is organized based on clan. Leadership is exercised by the head of the lineage, a male chosen on the basis of "seniority of generation" or

---

17. Ibid., 65.
18. Ibid., 218.
19. Ibid.
20. Ibid., 219.

"by seniority of age."[21] The head of the lineage exercises "political power through moral or ritual prestige, respect and honor."[22] Other forms of political leadership are chiefships comprising of several clans and kinships. Leaders are selected from the male "descendants of the founder of the chiefships for ritual reasons: only they can relate satisfactorily with the chiefly ancestors. Chiefs should be people of good moral reputation, prestige and material means."[23]

3. Centralized and authoritative political organization, practiced among the Banyoro of Uganda, is hierarchical in nature: all authority stems from the king down to the house elder of the family. "Between parents and children, but particularly between fathers and children, the relationship is one of superiority and subordination."[24] From this political structure the king is considered to be an embodiment of the community:

> The king's personal shortcomings and his strengths are not only his own but those of the whole population. Because they affect both the population and the land, the king has to ensure that he is always in good physical, ritual and spiritual condition."[25] To this effect, sacrifices are offered not only to the good health of the king but also to the entire land.[26]

Political leadership in African societies is designed to foster harmonious relationships in the universe in order to sustain the abundant life. Despite the fact that leadership is basically hierarchical, patrilineal, and authoritative, grassroots consultations play a critical role in promoting a smooth-running community. Rights and duties in political leadership form a central pillar in the community.

> In African chiefships and kingdoms, for instance, one of the primary functions of the chief or king is to entertain his nobles, converse with them, and thus learn wisdom and justice by consulting them on matters of state.... The leader also has tribute

21. Ibid., 220.
22. Ibid.
23. Ibid., 220–21.
24. Ibid., 223.
25. Ibid., 225.
26. Ibid.

regularly paid to him, so that in case of need he can provide for his subjects.[27]

Equally critical to the political organization is for a leader to promote dignity for humankind and nature. In Africa, dignity is defined both in positive and negative terms:

> Dignity means, of course, absence of want. It means wealth in crops, animals and children. It means the absence of disease and other social afflictions. It means there is practical evidence of abundant life. In terms of political leadership, dignity includes all of these qualities and more.[28]

Promoting dignity is the moral duty of a leader, who ought to be impeccable. Some kind of system of checks and balances must to be in place to ensure sustained responsibility and accountability. Whoever indulges in corruption, favoritism, making unjust judgments, or taking bribes is never tolerated.[29] In all of this, politics and religion play a critical role in the traditional African societies. Therefore powers from God, through the ancestors, are invoked by performing rituals and sacrifices for the well-being of the community.

Political leadership ensures that law and order are maintained. Disputes are settled through the courts. In traditional Africa, "the primary court is the community in which an individual lives and has immediate responsibilities and rights, whether this community is the family, the village or the age-set."[30] In the case of a family, the head of the household is entitled to resolve conflicts; and in the case of a village, the village leader assumes the role. Maintaining good relationships and communal solidarity is the main objective in settling disputes and redressing wrongs in the African traditional courts. In the process, the leader ought to exercise the art of listening to both sides prior to a judgment.[31] Although punishment is part of discharging justice, reconciliation remains the chief goal.[32]

It is worth noting that while settling disputes and discharging justice remain the major responsibility of the primary courts legal system, mo-

27. Ibid.
28. Ibid., 231.
29. Ibid.
30. Ibid., 236.
31. Ibid., 234.
32. Ibid., 241.

rality and religion are inseparable. Prior to settling personal and social disputes in court, the experience, customs and taboos, and legacy of the ancestors were often cited as the basis or an inspiration for good moral standards. The family spirits and God were invoked to assist in maintaining impartiality and fairness while ministering justice in traditional courts.[33] It was and still is believed that any social disorder in the UMUMTU bears a negative impact on the entire human community, while social harmony and tranquility enhances the abundant life. Adequate understanding of the African social milieu is critical to offering a better understanding of justice.

UMUMTU represents the full meaning of community. When developing a concept of justice, it is important to see how religion, ethics, morals, and politics are interrelated and integrated. And how these webs of relationships are ordered in UMUMTU is a precondition for a just and peaceful community. So, maintaining the right relationships in UMUMTU is a precondition for a good moral life.

In Africa, human dignity means enjoying the abundant life. Human dignity becomes a reality when vital forces are well-ordered in UMUMTU. Social disorder or injustice, however, is a result of the disruption of webs of relationships in UMUMTU and thus threatens human dignity. The goal of political leadership is to maintain these relationships in UMUMTU in order to promote abundant life and dignity. In other words, one can say that the subject matter of African justice is how actions and institutions contribute to promoting abundant life in the universe.

The image of UMUMTU consists of complex communal relationships. The sacred character of UMUMTU makes justice and peace one of the most sophisticated notions to explore in African religion, and a number of important points for inspiration can be retrieved from the African image of justice through UMUMTU. This complex image portrays the nature of justice as wholesomeness, integration, unity, pluralism, solidarity, interdependence, integrity, interrelationships, intrarelationships, and subsidiarity. The result of these interrelationships is peace, wholeness, harmony, balance, equilibrium, and cosmic moral order.

Furthermore, UMUMTU consists of the spiritual and religious ingredients of justice. As seen in part 1, the analysis of the contemporary social theorists demonstrated the lack of these crucial ingredients that are

---

33. Ibid., 235.

critical to a fuller understanding of justice and the enjoyment of greater peace. For example, stressing negative liberties and rights over positive liberties and rights renders the understanding of justice and peace inadequate. In UMUMTU, integral justice ought to include both of the negative and positive rights. Integral justice generates integral duties: positive and negative duties of justice. The image of UMUMTU seems to portray a fuller understanding of justice and greater peace. The essence of UMUMTU is all about the abundant life critical to living human dignity. Therefore, political leadership is evaluated by the way the abundant life is protected and promoted.

6 Biblical Narratives of Justice

Justice is essentially an abolitionist theory as much as egalitarianism is. Justice calls for the abolition of injustice; equality calls for the abolition of inequality; human rights call for an end to human rights abuses or deprivations, and peace calls for a resolution of conflicts or a diffusion of tensions.

From the previous discussions on justice and social theories in part 1, a question that comes to mind is whether any of the interpretations of justice described in part 1 are adequate in dealing with injustices in society. For example, Rawls, through the hypothetical method, believes that the principles enacted[1] are fair because the method is fair: people come together to decide how to live their lives. To do so, they have to set up social ventures or social arrangements. Justice is about how the basic structures of society are organized and how people distribute rights and duties, benefits and burdens. Rawls accords more importance to the first principle of justice than to the second: basic liberties enjoy a priority over social and economic rights. Rawls acknowledges the fact that the ordering of the principles would cause some form of inequalities when applied in a lexical order.[2] To foster justice as fairness in real life, a way has to be found to minimize the inequalities and maximize the benefits of the least advantaged. Liberal theory asserts that inequalities are justified by the principle of maximin[3] in so far as the benefits are maximized for the least advantaged individuals or groups. In so doing, the gap between the most advantaged and the least advantaged eventually narrows down. But how narrow is narrow? Or how narrow is the gap between the well-

---

1. These principles are as follows: "first, each person is to have an equal right to the most extensive scheme of equal basic liberty rights compatible with a similar scheme of liberties for others. Second, social and economic inequalities are to be arranged so that they are both (a) reasonably expected to be at every one's advantage, and (b) attached to positions open to all." (Rawls, *Theory of Justice*, 54)

2. Lexical ordering of principles means the first principle is more important than the second principle and, thus it enjoys the first priority when it comes to implementation.

3. *Maximin* means "to maximize the minimum."

off and the least well-off, which can be ethically and morally justifiable? The liberal theory is silent about it. It's worth remembering that Rawls, a proponent of social contract theory or liberalism, criticized Mill, a proponent of classical utilitarianism, for imposing on people or society ideas or ethical principles without being involved in determining such principles. Seemingly, liberalism attempts to offer an alternative answer to the flaws inherent in utilitarianism. However, liberalism is faced with one crucial problem: the way that the theory can narrow the gap between the least advantaged and the most advantaged was not satisfactorily demonstrated by Rawls.

One thing has to be clear: it's not the intention of Rawls to come up with a simple egalitarian society. The strength of liberalism lies in the equality of individual in exercising basic liberties. The problem with liberalism is that basic liberties are regarded from a negative rather than a positive perspective. This notion will be further developed later in the upcoming chapter.

Walzer (a communitarian), Nozick (a libertarian), and Iris Marion Young (a social feminist) have criticized Rawls for being insensitive to differences and particularities of the parties or individuals taking part in the social contract through the hypothetical method of the original position. Rawls's critics argue that a theory that history takes into account is needed to deal with the real people, real issues, real problems, and real solutions. Dealing with what really happened (history), however, does not necessarily tell us that whatever happened was right because of the way it happened. According to Nozickian view of justice, a good result proceeds from the right method and the right method precedes a good result. For example, something is just and good if the right method of acquiring and exchanging goods is followed. Equating history with rightness or wrongness (morality of justice) is the fallacy of our times.

Nozick's theory, in particular, shows the contrast between philanthropic charity and Christian charity. Nozick's emphasis on the individual's right to the acquisition and free exchange of goods or property, a process justified by a historical method, leaves room for some serious ethical and moral questions. Nozick believes that injustices resulting from acquisition or exchange should be addressed by the state through the principle of rectification. In other words, the state's primary responsibility is to protect individual rights to life, liberty, and private property and to address the injustices that occur in the process. Nozick, however, falls short in addressing the problems people face in seeking redress of injustices in judicial systems. What is the best thing can money buy? At times money can buy justice. In addition, Nozick believes that charity should have a place in libertarian society. To Nozick, charity, however, is not a morally binding obligation. Rather, charity is a philanthropic venture. In the next discussion, we will see how different biblical justice, *sedaqah*, is from Nozick's concept of justice and how closely justice is linked to charity.

NATURE AND SCOPE OF BIBLICAL JUSTICE

What does the Bible say about the notion of justice? How different is it from liberalism, libertarianism, feminism, utilitarianism, or communitarianism? We will now explore the nature of biblical justice both in the Old Testament and New Testament.

Justice and Agape

The libertarian view of justice is that the right method determines the just outcome; the right precedes the good and the good proceeds from the right. As seen earlier, this kind of justice theory has some serious flaws. From a biblical perspective, who is considered a just person? Or what are just actions like? What is a just society or community? A good number of biblical narratives cited from the Old and the New Testament will help us understand or grasp the nature of faith-based justice.

In the book of Job, justice is not only seen from the perspective of a person's relationship with Yahweh: "Let God weigh me in the scales of justice; thus will he know my innocence" (Job 31:6).[4] Rather, justice is about a host of other important things like land, harvest, servants, the poor, and the widow. Justice, *sedaqah*, results in peaceful harmony, *shalom*, within the individual person and the community when the right relationships with land, servants, the poor, and the widow are fostered:

> If I have eaten its produce without payment and grieved the hearts of its tenants; then let the thistles grow instead of wheat and noxious weeds instead of barley. . . . Had I refused justice to my manservant or to my maid, when they had a claim against me, what then should I do when rose up; what could I answer when he demanded an account? . . . If I have denied anything to the poor

---

4. All biblical references are to the New American Bible, Saint Joseph edition, unless otherwise noted.

> or allowed the eyes of the widow to languish while I ate my portion alone, with no share in it with the fatherless.
> (Job 31:39–40, 13–14, 16–17)

According to Ps 112, a just man is described as one who fears Yahweh and keeps Yahweh's commandments, and as one who is led to enjoy blessedness, happiness, riches, and wealth both for his family and his descendants. Trusting in Yahweh, one will never waver in the midst of bad news. By keeping Yahweh's commandments, one becomes honest, upright, merciful, tenderhearted, and virtuous. Honesty, uprightness, mercy, tenderness, and virtue translate into actions, which impact the community. "Lavishly, they give to the poor; their prosperity shall endure for ever; their horn shall be exalted in honor" (Ps 112:9).

On the social and the divine dimensions of justice, John R. Donahue comments:

> The double statement of justice enduring forever in the context of both possessing wealth and distributing it captures the biblical notion that the goods of this earth are the signs of the right relationship with Yahweh as well as the means to create harmony within the community.[5]

Furthermore, Ps 18:24–27 (JB) speaks of the reward to those who act justly:

> And Yahweh repays me as I act justly, as my purity is in his sight. Faithful you are with the faithful, blameless with the blameless, pure with the one who is pure, but crafty with the devious, you save a people that is humble and humiliate eyes that are haughty.[6]

Does justice guarantee the absence of suffering, pain, trials, or tribulations? Or is a just person subject to suffering or pain? Is a just person exempt from trials and tribulations? Can God repay a just person with suffering or pain? Experiences have shown that honest, upright, and just people do suffer. Why? Is it fair for good and just persons to suffer? Do we really understand God's justice? Job, the servant of God, though just and innocent, suffered. Is this the same God seen in Ps 112?

---

5. Donahue, "Biblical Perspectives on Justice," 70.

6. This excerpt from the Jerusalem Bible better expresses the "action" of a just man rather than simply describing his "righteousness" as in the American Bible.

Job lost everything: wealth, riches, prosperity, friends, and his life was wretched. Faced with this harsh situation, Job responds to Yahweh as follows:

> I know that you are all-powerful: what you conceive, you can perform. I am the man who obscured your designs with my empty-headed words. I have been holding forth on matters I cannot understand, on marvels beyond me and my knowledge. . . . I knew you then by hearsay; but now, having seen you with my own eyes, I retract all I have said, and in dust and ashes I repent.
> (Job 42:1–6 JB)

Job's friends, Eliphaz of Teman, Bildad of Shuah, and Zophar of Naamath, did not speak truthfully about Yahweh as Job did. What's this truth? Perhaps, these friends did not understand the ways of God. Donahue's remarks may help shed some light into the mystery of God's justice:

> The justice of God is both a gift and mystery, and the attempt to crystallize it by human standards can result in destroying the proper relation with Yahweh. To live justly is to rejoice in the good things of life and at the same time to be able to recognize that life is a gift even in the face of loss and destructiveness. To be just is to be open to the world as gift and God as mystery.[7]

Finally, Job came to grips with his own trials by speaking truthfully of Yahweh; his fortunes were restored and he was reunited with his family and his friends (Job 42:10–15).

Who is this mysterious and just God? Does God punish injustices? The Old Testament prophets proclaim Yahweh as just: "The Lord within her is just, who does no wrong; morning after morning he renders judgment unfailingly, at dawn" (Zeph 3:5).

Similarly, the writer of the book of Chronicles asserts the same idea about Yahweh:

> However, the commanders of Israel and the king humbled themselves, saying, "The Lord is just." When the Lord saw that they had humbled themselves, the word of the Lord came to Shemaiah: "Because they have humbled themselves I will not destroy them; I will give them some deliverance, and my wrath shall not be poured out upon Jerusalem through Shishak." (2 Chron 12:6–7)

---

7. Donahue, "Biblical Perspectives on Justice," 71.

Yahweh's justice includes punishment for infidelity to Yahweh's covenant, which demands that the marginalized be cared for:

> Woe to those who enact unjust statutes and who write oppressive decrees, depriving the needy of judgment and robbing my people's poor of their rights, making widows their plunder, and orphans their prey. What will you do on the day of punishment, when ruin comes from afar? (Isa 10:1–3a)

Yahweh's punishment of the sinner is regarded as the restoration to salvation:

> I will make of right a measuring line, of justice a level. Hail shall sweep away the refuge of lies, and waters shall flood the hiding place. Your covenant with death shall be cancelled and your pact with the nether world shall not stand (Isa 10:17–18).

Israel was punished through invasion, destruction, and captivity by the Assyrians. Yahweh allows such things to happen to remind Israel of its infidelity to the demands of the covenant relationship. However, the remnant stands as a reminder of Yahweh's mercy, compassion, love, and forgiveness. Justice is not only about punishment; it is also about the restoration and salvation:

> The remnant of Israel, the survivors of the house of Jacob, will no more lean upon him who struck them. Yes, the destruction he has decreed, the Lord, the God of hosts, will carry out within the whole land. Therefore thus says the Lord, the God of hosts: O my people, who dwell in Zion, do not fear the Assyrian, though he strikes you with a rod, and raises his staff against you. For only a brief moment more, and my anger shall be over; but them I will destroy in wrath. Then the Lord of hosts will raise against them a scourge such as struck Midian at the rock of Oreb; and he will raise his staff over the sea as he did against Egypt. On that day, his burden shall be taken from your shoulder, and his yoke shattered from your neck (Isa 10:20–27).

Just as Yahweh is merciful, loving, forgiving, compassionate, so too are those in covenant with Yahweh called to be merciful, loving, forgiving, compassionate. The measure he gives to us is also the measure one ought to dish out to others. Fidelity to the demands of the covenant calls Israel to be mindful of certain groups of people:

> You shall not molest or oppress an alien, for you were once aliens yourselves in the land of Egypt. You shall not wrong any widow or orphan. If ever you wrong them and they cry out to me, I will surely hear their cry. My wrath will flare up, and I will kill you with a sword; then your own wives will be widows, and your children orphans. (Exod 22:20–23)

By the same token, Donahue notes, "characteristic of all strands of Israel's traditions is concern for the widow, the orphan, the poor and the sojourner in the land."[8]

Living justly results in a blessing for those who are faithful to Yahweh's covenant demand to help those in need, including both members of the community as well as strangers:

> At the end of every third year you shall bring out all the tithes of your produce for that year and deposit them in community stores, the Levite who has no share in the heritage with you, and also the alien, the orphan and the widow who belong to your community, may come and eat their fill; so that the Lord, your God, may bless you in all that you undertake. (Deut 14:28–29)

However, injustice calls for judgment and punishment. The prophet Amos, one of the staunchest prophets of his time, was against social injustices when the rich exploited the poor:

> Thus says the Lord: For three crimes of Israel, and for four, I will not revoke my word; because they sell the just man for silver, and the poor man for a pair of sandals. They trample the heads of the weak into the dust of the earth, and force the lowly out of the way. Son and father go to the same prostitute, profaning my holy name. (Amos 2:6–7)

Religion and worship ought to translate into a concrete action. In Israel, at the time of Amos, however, religion was more and more reduced to legalism, externalism, and ritualism. Yahweh's response was undoubtedly prompt and timely:

> I hate, I spurn your feasts, I take no pleasure in your solemnities. Your cereal offerings I will not accept, nor consider your stall-fed peace offerings. Away with your noisy songs! I will not listen to the melodies of your harps. But if you would offer me holocausts, then

---

8. Ibid., 73.

let justice surge like water, and goodness like an unfailing stream.
(Amos 5:21–24)

Donahue makes an excellent comment regarding the wholesomeness of justice:

> The imagery here is striking. One function of the cult (feasts and solemn assemblies) was to pray for the water and flowing streams which would assure fertility and hence life to the land. By comparing justice and righteousness with water and a stream, Amos, speaking in the name of Yahweh, shows that without justice the totality of life is barren.[9]

Throughout the Old Testament literature, while the core meaning of justice, *sedaqah*, remains unchanged, there have been some transformations of the term during the intertestamental period (the period between the exile and the New Testament). *Sedaqah*, as fidelity to the demands of the covenant relationship, means that Israel was called to be compassionate to the concerns and needs of the four groups of people: the poor, widows, orphans, and aliens (sojourners/strangers). During this period, there was a "shift in language whereby *sedaqah* means almsgiving or care for the poor."[10] The book of Tobit sheds some light into such a transformation:

> Prayer and fasting are good, but better than either is almsgiving accompanied by righteousness. A little with righteousness is better than abundance with wickedness. It is better to give alms than to store up gold; for almsgiving saves one from death and expiates every sin. Those who regularly give alms shall enjoy a full life, but those habitually guilty of sin are their own worst enemies.
> (Tob 12:8–10)

The biblical meaning of charity (*agape*) is intrinsic to justice (*sedaqah*), as opposed to the Nozickian view of charity as something extrinsic to justice. The parable of the good Samaritan calls the believer to charity: love of neighbor as justice.[11] In expressing the fidelity to Christian discipleship, doing charity is the right action or it is a good thing to do. The parable of the good Samaritan stresses that helping the needy is an act of love. At the end of the parable Jesus makes an imperative state-

---

9. Ibid., 75. A similar message is echoed in Jer 22:13, 15–16 and in Isa 58:6–7.

10. Ibid., 79.

11. Regarding the connection of justice and charity, see Msoka, *Basic Human*, 119–22. Also see Msoka, "Cosmotheandrization of Human Rights," 84–85.

ment, "Go and do likewise" (Luke 10: 37). Loving the neighbor is morally binding because it is an expression of Christian discipleship. Donahue's comments:

> This development represents a very important facet of biblical thought which was obscured by later distinctions between justice and charity. Concern for the poor and a desire to lessen the inequality between rich and poor either individually or collectively, in a biblical perspective, should not proceed simply from a love for a compassion with the suffering of others, but is rooted in claims of justice, i.e., how one can be faithful to the Lord who has given the goods of the earth as common possession of all and be faithful to others in the human community who have equal claim to these goods.[12]

The shift in language was a preparation for the transition from the Old Testament to the New Testament era as echoed in Jesus's teaching on justice. Throughout the New Testament, justice is centered on Jesus Christ. Jesus's fellowship or relationship with the outcast and sinners in society mirrors or echoes the understanding of justice in the Old Testament as a concern for the poor, the orphan, the widow, and the alien (Mark 2:17). In the Gospel of Mathew, justice or righteousness (*dikaiosyne* in Greek), which leads to a blessing or the inheritance of the kingdom, is measured by the way one treats the marginal: "For I was hungry and you gave me food, I was thirsty and you gave me drink, a stranger and you welcome me, naked and you clothed me, ill and you care for me, in prison and you visited me" (Matt 25:35–36).

Donahue reminds us that understanding justice in the Old Testament, *sedaqah*, is critical to understanding justice in the New Testament, *dikaiosyne*. "As in the Old Testament the marginal ones become the touchstone for the doing of justice."[13] Christ Jesus is the embodiment of justice. The followers of Jesus in the Gospel of Matthew could not comprehend the connection between social justice and the person of Jesus Christ, so he explained to them, "And the king will say to them in reply, Amen, I say to you, whatever you did for one of these least brothers for mine, you did it for me" (Matt 25:40).

---

12. Donahue, "Biblical Perspectives on Justice," 84–85.
13. Ibid., 105.

A MACROTHEORY OF JUSTICE

Justice and Faith

Because biblical justice is basically about fulfilling the right relationships with one another, and particularly with the marginalized, as an expression of fidelity to the demands of the covenant, linking justice to faith is essential. To some, faith-based justice is foreign territory, while to others it is an interesting area to explore. This section will explain the connection of faith and biblical justice and how such a connection is important to peace in the present world and the world to come.

In the Reformation period, justice and faith were contentious theological issues, and perhaps they still are today. Exploring justice and faith in Pauline writings is complex because Pauline language can be metaphorical. Often, in the writings, God's justice is associated with the death and resurrection of Christ:

> But now the righteousness of God has been manifested apart from the law, though testified to by the law and the prophets, the righteousness of God through faith in Jesus Christ for all who believe. For there is no distinction; all have sinned and are deprived of the glory of God. They are justified freely by his grace through the redemption in Christ Jesus. (Rom 3:21–22)

Paul links Christ's death and resurrection in the New Testament to the exodus event of liberation in the Old Testament. Christ's death and resurrection is seen as a new Passover: freedom from slavery in Egypt is associated with freedom from sin through Christ's redemption. As such, the history of salvation is one of sanctification:

> I am speaking in human terms because of the weaknesses of your nature. For just as you presented the parts of your bodies as slaves to impurity and to lawlessness for lawlessness, so now present them as slaves to righteousness for sanctification. For when you were slaves of sin, you were free from righteousness. . . . But now that you have been freed from sin and have become slaves of God, the benefit that you have leads to sanctification, and its end is eternal life. (Rom 6:19–22)

Another effect of Christ's death and resurrection is reconciliation:

> Indeed, if, while we were enemies, we were reconciled to God through the death of his Son, how much more, once reconciled, will we be saved by his life? Not only that, but we also boast of

God through our Lord Jesus Christ, through whom we have now received reconciliation. (Rom 5:10–11)

Peace (*shalom*) is considered the fruit of justice (*sedaqah*), echoing the words of the prophet Isaiah, "Justice will bring about peace; right will produce calm and security. My people will live in peaceful country, in secure dwellings and quiet resting places" (Isa 32:17).[14] Donahue comments: "When we recall that in the Old Testament one effect of the realization of the justice of God is that of peace (shalom), wholeness and harmony are to reign, we can see that the reconciled world is a world where peace and harmony are to prevail."[15]

According to the Apostle Peter, justice and justification through the cross and resurrection of Christ are closely tied. And the effect of Christ's cross is justification as freedom from sin and freedom for God and for others: "He himself bore our sins in his body on the cross, so that, free from sin, we might live in righteousness. By his wounds you have been healed. For you had gone astray like sheep, but you have now returned to the shepherd" (1 Pet 2:24–25).

Paul argues along the same lines as Peter. "Freed from sin, you have become slaves of righteousness" (Rom 6:18). Peter's and Paul's understanding of freedom reflects on Christ's mission statement as stated in his inaugural discourse in the synagogue: "the Spirit of the Lord is upon me to preach the good news to the poor and liberation to captives" (Luke 4:18–19).

Justification has a social implication when one considers that sin affects not only the individual person; rather, personal sin has a negative effect on the others and the world. By the same token, personal justification and freedom through Christ's redemption ought to have a positive effect on the social order:

> For you were called for freedom, brothers. But do not use this freedom as an opportunity for the flesh; rather, serve one another through love. For the whole law is fulfilled in one statement, namely, "You shall love your neighbor as yourself." But if you go on biting and devouring one another, beware that you are not consumed by one another. (Gal 5:13)

14. For further information about the interrelation between justice and peace see Msoka, *Basic Human Rights*, 120. Also see Msoka, "Cosmotheandrization of Human Rights," 85.

15. Donahue, "Biblical Perspectives on Justice," 93–94.

By sanctification, reconciliation, and justification, a believer in Christ becomes open to God, to people, and to the world. Freedom from the flesh means freedom in the Spirit, and through that freedom, one enjoys the fruits of the Spirit: "The fruit of the Spirit is love, joy, peace, patience, kindness, generosity, faithfulness, gentleness, self-control" (Gal 5:22–23). Donahue notes:

> Sin is then the desire and tendency of man to live for himself alone in a world of social and religious isolation; it is the equivalent of living according to the flesh. Freedom from sin is then found when the believer sees himself as one ransomed, as one who does not belong simply to himself, but lives free of care, and lives open to the Lord.[16]

In addition, Paul stresses that freedom for Christ must entail freedom from the law. Paul's interpretation of freedom from the law is twofold: first, it entails Gentiles' freedom from following the Jewish law, customs, and traditions: "If you, though, a Jew, are living like a Gentile and not like the Jew, how can you compel the Gentiles to live like Jews?" (Gal 2:14b). The second sense is that freedom from the law is freedom from legalism, namely, the idea that justification can be achieved by simply being obedient to religious prescriptions and regulations, as Donahue observes:

> Paul sees in legalism an exclusiveness which would make Christianity into a set of norms and customs, rather than a gift to be shared. Legalism would make the Church simply into a society [corporation] rather than into a community whereby membership transcends all norms and social custom.[17]

Freedom from legalism to freedom for the love of God and of neighbor is the essence of Christian teaching. Love fulfills the law. "Owe nothing to anyone, except to love one another; for the one who loves another has fulfilled the law" (Rom 13:8). The Ten Commandments can be summed up as loving God and loving the neighbor as you love yourself. "Love does no evil to the neighbor; hence, love is the fulfillment of the law" (Rom 13:10). To Paul, freedom from the law is also freedom from death. In seeing Christ's resurrection as victory over sin and death, Christians have the hope that faith in Christ brings the hope of eternal life. "For wages of

---

16. Ibid., 96.
17 .Ibid., 97.

sin is death, but the gift of God is eternal life in Christ Jesus our Lord" (Rom 6:23).

Justice and Hope

The Old Testament writings speak of the fulfillment of justice at the end of time. The Prophet Isaiah foretells the messianic times in which the New Jerusalem will be revealed:

> No longer shall violence be heard of in your land, or plunder and ruin within your boundaries. You shall call your walls "salvation" and your gates "praise." No longer shall be the sun be your light by day, nor the brightness of the moon shine upon you by night; the Lord shall be your light forever, your God shall be your glory. No longer shall your sun go down, or your moon withdraw, for the Lord will be your light forever, and the days of your mourning shall be at an end. Your people shall be just, they shall always posses the land. (Isa 60:18–21a)

Eschatological justice is about reward, which is peace and happiness, and punishment (pain) due to the lack of fulfillment or satisfaction:

> Many of those who sleep in the dust of the earth shall awake; some shall live forever, others shall be an everlasting horror and disgrace. But the wise shall shine brightly like the splendor of the firmament, and those who lead the many to justice shall be like the stars forever. (Dan 12:2–3)

The Sermon on the Mount, Christ's message of "blessedness," is not only meant for the present moment; rather, the message sends a signal that blessedness and beatific vision are the complete fulfillment of justice in the messianic times or at the end of time: "Blessed are they who hunger and thirst for righteousness, for they will be satisfied" (Matt 5:6). The kingdom of God is already here, and yet its fulfillment will be at the end of time. Jesus begins his public ministry with this message, "The time has come . . . and the kingdom of God is close at hand. Repent, and believe the Good News" (Mark 1:15).

Full realization of justice has something to do with the perfect alignment of the human will with the divine will. Or it is about the perfect harmony of the human will with the divine will. In fact, the full realization of justice results in peace bonded in love: the human will ties a knot with the divine will so that the two wills are no longer two, but one will.

Consequently, we shall be as loving as God is love; we shall be as just as God is just; we shall be as good as God is good; we shall be as perfect as God is perfect; and as peaceful as God is peaceful. Donahue remarks, "Therefore, in eschatological thought not only are the faithful 'justified' at the end of time, but God himself is shown to be just and faithful."[18]

In the biblical tradition, where fidelity to the demands of the covenant is central, *the justice of God shapes a just person* and a just person shapes a just society. In other words, the rightness and the goodness of personal and social actions are shaped by the just actions of God. A just God precedes a just person, and a just person proceeds from a just God who is always faithful to the covenant.

A libertarian view of justice stresses that the outcome of transactions or an exchange of goods is just and therefore good provided the process of distribution governing justice is rightly followed. In other words, the right and the good are intimately linked. However, as a libertarian historical method has shown, following the process correctly does not necessarily yield the best results. It seems to be an open-ended process. Therefore, history and ethics are not one and the same thing.

Biblical justice maintains that something is just and therefore good not because it is right. Rather, it is *right and good* because it is *just*. We are called to be just because God is just and faithful to the covenant. Hence, justice is primarily rooted in the new covenant, Christ, the justice of God. In biblical justice, God is the point of departure because the covenant was made with his own initiative, or the actions of compassion, love, and mercy. Furthermore, God is the point of arrival because the complete fulfillment of human justice is God: in God everything is perfectly right, just, and absolutely good.

---

18. Ibid., 81.

Conclusion to Part 2

The focus of the biblical justice tradition is fidelity to the demands of the covenantal relationship between God and God's people. This relationship was fully sealed in Christ with his own precious blood. The demands of such a relationship involve the love of God and of neighbor, particularly of the poor, the widow, the orphan, and the stranger. The parable of the Good Samaritan is a demonstration of this great demand. From a biblical perspective, an integral justice consists of three ingredients or threads: charity, faith, and hope. Therefore, justice is intimately connected to charity, faith, and hope.

Justice is not determined by the procedural methods of distribution as Nozick proposed. Rather, the right distributions of goods, power, and so on, are rooted in an understanding of the justice of God. Furthermore, the good is not determined by the consequences of our actions, as Mill proposed in his theory of classical utilitarianism. Rather, the good is determined by the rightness of our actions. The justice of God as portrayed in the Bible is the foundation for good conduct and for a just society, unlike Walzer's proposal of justice as a product of social construction or a product of social contract. A contract is just insofar as it reflects the justice of God: human dignity is the basis of equal treatment and equal protection. These claims of justice generate the duties of justice, as will be discussed in part 3, chapter 8.

The justice of God is realized in historical stages, with the hope of being fully realized at the end of history, in which the human will ties a knot with the divine will. Unlike the liberal and libertarian view of justice with an emphasis on negative liberty, biblical justice is threaded or integral: it includes not only liberation and freedom from sin but also freedom for God and for individuals.

Biblical justice shares some similarity with African cultural narratives, UMUMTU and ORUM. Relationship is the factor of commonality between the two narratives. The convergence of these two narratives forms a very rich understanding of macrojustice. Chapter 7 offers the ethical and moral significance of the theory of macrojustice. Chapter 8 offers methodological considerations for a paradigmatic theory of justice.

Part 3

Towards a Paradigmatic Theory of Justice

In part 1, I discussed the nature and scope of selected social theories and identified their strengths and limitations. In view of these limitations, the rationale for seeking a new understanding of justice was established. In part 2, I sought the possible sources for constructing a macrotheory of justice, namely the African perspective of justice, UMUMTU, and the biblical perspective of justice, *sedaqah*. In the discussions, similarities and dissimilarities between the two approaches were drawn: The element of relationship with God and humankind is the common ground for both sources of justice. In contrast with *sedaqah*, however, UMUMTU encompasses not only the notions of God and humankind in the relationship, but also nature and its sacred character. Furthermore, for UMUMTU, the notion of humankind connotes the physical and the spiritual world, namely the living, the living dead, and the unborn. Finally, in chapter 6, a contrast was made regarding the selected social theories seen in chapter 1. The authors of the contemporary theories of justice considered humankind as the sole bearer of justice, and the concept of humankind did not encompass its spiritual element and the unborn. Therefore, a macrotheory of justice, which will be all-encompassing, is critical to addressing the issues of justice facing both humankind and nature.

Introduction

Part 3 has two chapters. Chapter 7 will show more directly the ethical significance of a macrotheory of justice by comparing it with the Catholic Church's interpretation and application of the biblical notion of justice. Chapter 8 will consider a methodology for constructing a macrotheory of justice.

7 The Ethical and Moral Significance of a Macrotheory of Justice

The scope of Catholic interpretation and application of biblical justice will now be examined. The critique will focus on the following works: "Economic Justice for All" (1986), by the U.S. Catholic Bishops; "Justice in the World" (1971), by the Synod of Catholic Bishops; and "Deeper Evangelization in the Third Millennium" (2002), by the Catholic Bishops of the Association of Member Episcopal Conferences in Eastern Africa (AMECEA).

A CRITICAL EXAMINATION OF CATHOLIC INTERPRETATION AND APPLICATION OF A BIBLICAL PERSPECTIVE OF JUSTICE

The pastoral letter, "Economic Justice for All," published in 1986 by the U.S. Catholic Conference of Bishops, maintains that civil and political rights, as well as social and economic rights, are critical to a life of dignity.[1] In defending this position, the bishops employ the biblical perspective of justice as the basis for enjoying equal economic justice for all in the United States of America.[2] The bishops further analyze biblical justice into the three main categories of commutative justice, distributive justice, and social justice, or contributive justice.[3]

First, they define commutative justice as the principle that governs or regulates human relationships between individuals or between groups in making transactions, contracts, or agreements.[4] The parties in question

---

1. U.S. Catholic Bishops, "Economic Justice for All," 598, nos. 80–82.

2. Ibid., 586, nos. 35–44.

3. The U.S. bishops used the neoscholastic philosophy rooted in Thomism in interpreting and applying biblical justice to economic justice. It's worth noting that neoscholastic philosophy may not be appealing to all people of all places, times, and cultures. On this note see Curran, *Catholic Social Teaching*, 189. The need for a new approach to justice is critical to a deeper understanding of peace.

4. Ibid., 595, no. 69.

ought to treat one another with equal respect and dignity. Human dignity can be threatened or violated when relationships do not take into account the ethical values of equality, fairness, and respect.

Second, they define distributive justice as the principle that governs or regulates relationships of governments and their people. This type of justice demands that governments and other institutions put in place all the necessary measures and legal guarantees to address any violation of human dignity (equality, fairness, and respect) resulting from transactions, contracts, agreements, or dealing with people whose "basic material needs are unmet."[5]

Third, social justice, or contributive justice, governs relationships of people within their social institutions. This type of justice demands that all people must be empowered to participate actively in social life and contribute to create the necessary conditions (political and economic institutions) for the flourishing of the common good.[6] Furthermore, contributive justice addresses those questions, challenges, issues, or problems that can hinder people, particularly the poor, the weak, and the marginalized, from becoming active participants in socioeconomic and political life and securing such things as a quality education and employment. Contributing factors to this situation are the lack of the necessary empowerment, opportunities, or resources. Also, contributive justice addresses those challenges facing governments and other institutions from providing the necessary means, protections, policies, or conditions for socioeconomic and political well-being.

These dimensions of justice are intimately interrelated, integrated, and therefore, are interdependent.[7] The liberal and libertarian views of justice, however, do not seriously consider the ethical and moral interrelation and interdependence of these three dimensions of justice. Based on the notion of the minimal state, which calls for less government involvement in social life in order to reduce public spending, Nozick considers commutative justice more important than distributive justice and contributive justice.[8] For Nozick, social action or government intervention is ethically justified through the principle of rectification of injustices when

---

5. Ibid., 595, no. 70.
6. Ibid., 595, no. 71.
7. See Msoka, *Basic Human Rights*, 122.
8. See *Justice and Libertarianism*, chap. 3 of this book.

the holdings or the goods in question are not historical. In other words, the intervention is legitimate if the goods in question did not follow the principles of justice in the acquisition of goods or the principle of justice in free exchange of such goods.[9] For Nozick, all justice is reduced to commutative justice.

Distributive justice demands that all the basic social institutions have to be in place to ensure that all people enjoy or exercise their basic rights and fulfill their basic duties. To some extent, distributive justice and contributive justice have been given some attention in Rawls's theory of justice, unlike the Nozickian theory of justice. Rawls's has been credited with voicing the need for active social participation in choosing the principles of justice through the method of the original position. However, for Iris Marion Young and others, the use of the words "men" or "he" instead of "women" or "she" in Rawls's theory makes it seem as if women were not considered as an important part in the process of choosing the principles of justice. The lack of inclusive language in Rawls's method of the original position was seen by feminists as unfair because it ignored the particularity of individuals. [10]

Clearly, the notion of equal social and economic rights is not the top priority in Rawls's theory of justice as fairness. He, however, justified the existence of these rights under the difference principle by proposing some form of socioeconomic rights for the least advantaged through the maximization of the minimum strategy.[11] If one goes by this provision, it would mean that the life of the worst-off will always be heavily dependent on the well-off. It is worth noting basic justice demands for more than the difference principle and that distributive justice demands that the least advantaged people be accorded sufficient empowerment to liberate themselves from an extreme economic inequality. It is for this reason that the U.S. bishops maintained that all the three forms of justice are critical to

---

9. Lebacqz offers unfair criticism against Nozick in saying that "Nozick offers no room for the possibility that the current distributions are primae facie evidence of unfairness." Nozick does talk about the way to deal with unfair distributions by proposing the third principle of rectification of injustices. For clarification on this issue see *Justice and Libertarianism*, chap. 3 of this book. On the unfair criticism against Nozick, see Lebacqz, *Justice in an Unjust World*, 157.

10. See *Feminist Critique of Liberalism*, chap. 1.

11. See similar observations made by Karen Lebacqz, *Six Theories of Justice*, 37.

protecting human dignity: commutative justice, distributive justice, and contributive justice.

Michael Walzer's theory of justice advocates for the distribution of goods to members because they share a similar social understanding of these goods.[12] Hence, strangers are excluded from enjoying these social goods. Walzer argues that in order to avoid domination and tyranny and promote social equality there is a need to extend membership to strangers (refugees and immigrants) through the principle of mutual aid. However, Walzer admits that it is hard to provide a solid philosophical basis for the principle of mutual aid.[13]

Mill's greatest happiness principle takes into account the greatest happiness of all people. The problem with this theory is that the dignity or worthiness of the human person is extrinsic to the moral subject; human dignity is totally dependent on the way a person's actions contribute to the greatest happiness of all people (the net balance). Furthermore, Mill does not offer any provision on how the dignity of every person, particularly the weak and the vulnerable, would be protected by the utility principle, and it is unclear how the greatest happiness can trickle down to individual people. Most importantly, Mill prioritizes actions and their consequences over the human person as the moral subject.[14]

Biblical justice regards human dignity as an intrinsic value to the human person and not an extrinsic one as Mill suggests. A defense of every person's dignity, especially the weak, the poor, and the voiceless, is central in the Christian theory of justice. The U.S. bishops stressed that the preferential option for the poor demonstrates the fidelity to the demands of the covenant and strongly affirmed that it "is central priority for policy choice."[15]

The *imago Dei* theme has been featured prominently in the U.S. bishops' defense of human dignity. However, little attention has been paid to the relationship of humankind and nature (both animate and inanimate) in interpreting biblical justice.[16] Because integrity and uprightness are

---

12. See *Justice and Communitarianism*, chapter 4 of this book.

13. Ibid.

14. Curran, *Catholic Social Teaching*, 81.

15. U.S. Catholic Bishops, "Economic Justice for All," p. 637, no. 260.

16. The notion of ecological justice is present in some sections of the U.S. bishops' pastoral letter. However, it is unorganically developed (see p. 586, no. 34, and p. 663, nos. 362–63). Please note that ecological justice has been completely dropped from the moral

always referred to human persons, justice and peace are always associated with these persons only.[17] The cosmos is the cradle of humankind and a source of our livelihood. Moreover, no one can really demand economic justice without considering the critical role played by our planet earth. And without knowing the cosmos as God's reflection, it is almost impossible to care for it responsibly. Lack of the ecological ethics has often led to an inadequate development of ecological justice. To this effect, the U.S. bishops have called for a development of such ethics:

> All people on this globe share a common ecological environment that is under increasing pressure. Depletion of soil, water, and other natural resources endangers the future. Pollution of the air and water threatens the delicate balance of the biosphere on which future generations will depend. The resources of the earth have been created by God for the benefit of all, and we who are alive today hold them in trust. This is a challenge to develop a new ecological ethic that will help shape a future that is both just and sustainable.[18]

In African religion, nature is integral to UMUMTU and ORUM. Therefore, the interpretation of biblical justice enriched by African cultural narratives offers a constructive African Christian ecological ethics.

Some Western feminists maintain that love, marriage, sex, and procreation are a separate reality.[19] Some African feminists argue that love, marriage, sex, and procreation ought to be inseparable.[20] Biblically, love and justice are inseparable. Therefore, procreation through marital relationship is the right way to express sexual love. On the cultural front, there seems to be conflicting views between patriarchy and matriarchy. Oduyoye suggests that the values of both patriarchy and matriarchy can be incorporated and integrated to enrich the family because children need to be nurtured with the values in both cultural systems.[21] In general, feminists call for social inclusion of women into politics, economics, public policy, and religion. Christian justice demands that all people take an active part in social life, especially in caring for the marginalized,

---

priorities of the U.S. Catholic Bishops.

17. Clobus, *Environmental Care*, 65.
18. U.S. Catholic Bishops, "Economic Justice for All," 581, no. 12.
19. See *Justice, Feminism, and Liberalism*, chapter 1 of this book.
20. Ibid.
21. Ibid.

both in the private and public domains.²² The call for inclusion into various domains of life is best expressed through the cultural narratives of UMUMTU and ORUM.

As seen in *Anarchy, State, and Utopia*, Nozick's libertarian view of justice depicts a narrow window of the redistribution of goods to people in need as an act of philanthropy and not as an act of justice.²³ Hence, a Nozickian notion of charity is not grounded in the principle of basic justice that demands moral responsibility on the part of the charity-giver because one is charitable at one's own liberty. In contrast, the wholesome understanding of biblical justice is intimately connected to charity, faith, and hope.²⁴ The U.S. bishops succeeded in making a fundamental link between justice and charity and maintaining that charity is integral to justice,²⁵ echoing the African cultural narratives of justice, UMUMTU and ORUM.

In "Justice in the World," the 1971 Synod of Bishops expressed the need for greater justice in the world faced with domination, oppression, and the abuses of human rights. The synod believed that addressing these problems is central to the church's mission:

> Action on behalf of justice and participation in the transformation of the world fully appear to us as a constitutive dimension of the preaching of the Gospel, or, in other words, of the Church's mission for the redemption of the human race and its liberation from every oppressive situation.²⁶

The synod accounted for "forces" geared towards universal human solidarity. These forces are rooted in awareness of full basic equality as well as the human dignity of all: "since men are members of the same human family, they are indissolubly linked with one another in the one destiny of the whole world, in the responsibility for which they all share."²⁷ Based on these forces, the synod noted that people have now seen the need to

---

22. Ibid.
23. See *Justice and Libertarianism*, chapter 2 of this book.
24. See *African Cultural Narratives of Justice*, chapter 6 of this book.
25. U.S. Catholic Bishops, "Economic Justice for All," 588, no. 39.
26. Synod of Bishops, "Justice in the World," 289.
27. Ibid.

protect our planet (air, water, and the nature resources) for the good of all.[28]

The synod also warns about the dangers of the arms race at the expense of people's economic development, particularly of the less developed nations. The right to development was singled out as the only means of liberation from domination and oppression by fulfilling the "fundamental human rights upon which the aspirations of individuals and nations are based."[29] Given this crucial situation, the synod believed that the church ought to address those concerns in the light of Word of God.

From the perspectives of the Old Testament, the synod took up the theme of the God as "the liberator of the oppressed and the defender of the poor."[30] The synod tied together the theme of liberation to that of faith and justice: "it is only in the observance of the duties of justice that God is truly recognized as the liberator of the oppressed."[31] On the New Testament, the synod maintained that the justice of God was fully revealed and fulfilled in Christ (Luke 6:21–23), who identified himself with the least of his brethren (Matt 25:40).[32] The synod maintained that there is a close connection between justice and love: "Christian love of neighbor and justice cannot be separated. For love implies an absolute demand for justice, namely recognition of the dignity and rights of one's neighbor. Justice attains its inner fullness only in love."[33] Most importantly, justice and love ought to be expressed in action for the church to gain credibility with the world.[34] Finally, the synod reiterated that the mission of the hierarchical church is religious and that its mission is not to "offer concrete solutions in the social, economic, and political spheres for justice in the world. [Its] mission involves defending and promoting the dignity and fundamental rights of the human person."[35] The nonhierarchical church members as "members of society" have the same right and duty to promote the common good as do other citizens."[36] In contrast to the U.S.

28. Ibid.
29. Ibid., 290.
30. Ibid., 293.
31. Ibid.
32. Ibid.
33. Ibid.
34. Ibid.
35. Ibid., 294.
36. Ibid.

Conference of Catholic Bishops, who took up the theme of creation, liberation, covenant, and redemption, the synod took up the theme of liberation as a point of departure. Unlike the U.S. bishops' "Economic Justice for All," the Synod of Bishops' "Justice in the World," however, lacks the analytical dimensions of the biblical justice.

The question now is: how does the church do her mission in the name of justice? The synod affirmed that the church should bear witness to justice by being just herself and acting justly within herself (intrajustice). Just remuneration to church employees, encouraging active participation by women in the issues affecting the church and society, and the lifestyle of all must be seen in the ways that take the needs of the poor seriously.[37] The way the church witnesses to justice makes her more credible in the eyes of the world.[38] Furthermore, education for justice is paramount, and it must aim at educating humankind holistically against the forces of individualism and more and more focus on the social dimension of the human person: "but education demands a renewal of heart, a renewal based on the recognition of sin in its individual and social manifestations."[39]

Education for justice must start in the family, as the basic cell of society and the content of education "involves the respect for the person and for his dignity."[40] The synod's universal aim is to deal with the issues affecting the entire human family. In meeting the duties of justice, the solidarity of churches and international organizations is critical. On the international front, governments are called upon to ratify the United Nations' Declaration of Human Rights for those which have not done so.[41] Because the right to development is critical to liberation, the richer nations are called to assist the poor nations by granting preferential treatment for the manufactured goods of the latter to gain entry into the markets of the former.[42] Although the synod did not provide critical analysis of biblical justice as the U.S. bishops did, nevertheless, all the major implications of justice (in personal, sociopolitical, and economic domains) have been examined. Most importantly, the synod emphasized

37. Ibid., 295.
38. Ibid.
39. Ibid., 296.
40. Ibid.
41. Ibid., 298.
42. Ibid.

that faith, love, and justice, are intimately related, echoing the factors of interrelationship and integrity in the matters of holistic justice as seen in the African concept of justice, UMUMTU, which includes the protection of our planet and the natural resources as a matter of justice. This concept was hardly developed by the synod, however.

Respect for fundamental human rights as an issue of justice is grounded in the dignity or sacredness of the human person, as described in the creation narratives (Gen 2:26–27). Creation is the starting point for the theory of justice according to the U.S. bishops' document. This approach, however, is lacking in the Synod of Bishops' document. Hence, the approach to justice by the synod is inadequate.

In *Justice in an Unjust World: Foundations for a Christian Approach to Justice*, Karen Lebacqz complimented the U.S. Catholic Bishops for succeeding to offer a broader understanding of justice (commutative, distributive, and contributive) than the narrower understanding of justice (commutative) Nozick offered in *Anarchy, State, and Utopia*. Lebacqz is, however, critical of the U.S. Catholic Bishops' approach to justice in "Economic Justice for All" when the starting point of justice is the primary theme of creation and covenant rather than the theme of liberation:

> The Bishops stress creation and covenant as primary biblical themes. I stress covenant, but within the context of liberation. Because I begin with injustices, I cannot assume the coherence of the interests of all parties, as the Bishops do. I find not one word on justice, but two: different words spoken to the oppressed and to the oppressor.[43]

Lebacqz's vivid style of presenting biblical narratives of justice in the context of liberation and the covenant is worth noting and is rewarding. However, Lebacqz still thinks that the story of creation is insignificant in understanding justice: "injustice originates with violations of the responsibilities of the covenant. Injustice is wrong relationship."[44] Lebacqz further maintains that the biblical theme of liberation should be a starting point for the path towards justice. Lebacqz starts out with the history of the Israelites being oppressed in Egypt. If justice requires living out right relationships with God and with each other, then the rupture of justice began precisely with wrong relationships with God by the sin of Adam

---

43. Lebacqz, *Justice in an Unjust World*, 158.
44. Ibid., 153.

and Eve in the garden of Eden. Wrong relationships with God paved the way to distorted human relationships. Oppression is basically a manifestation of a ruptured justice. Therefore, the path to the restoration of justice or the correction of injustices must start with the biblical themes of creation, covenant, and redemption through Christ Jesus, the justice of God. Lebacqz's method of linking justice simply to the biblical theme of liberation, though in the context of the covenant, but de-linking it from creation is like placing the cart in front of the horse. The U.S. bishops are quite right in their approach in connecting justice to creation and finally to the covenant.[45] Rob Clobus argues along the same lines: "the creation story took shape long after the Jewish nation had emerged."[46]

The African cultural narrative of justice, UMUMTU and ORUM, portrays a network of the numerous threads, which link God, humankind, and nature to each other. The connection of these threads to each other to produce the image of integrity, unity, and solidarity and wholeness is a better approach to justice than that of the U.S. bishops. From the image of the African notion of justice, liberation from injustices is intimately linked to creation. By linking justice to the covenant, right relationships with God and with each other can be restored, which were disrupted by the fall of Adam and Eve, as illustrated by the creation story.

The stress on liberation both from personal and social sin as the origin of all the forms of injustices (domination, oppression, tyranny, and so on) does not loom large in Lebacqz's notion of justice. Lack of such understanding makes the path to greater justice and peace virtually impossible. Therefore, tracing the primary source of injustices from the biblical story of the covenant rather than from the biblical story of creation is inappropriate. Most importantly, by virtue of their inner logic, justice and human dignity are intimately connected. Tying liberation from injustices to the story of creation rather than simply to the liberation of injustices from Egypt would show that oppression is morally wrong and therefore sinful because it undermines the dignity of the human person created in

---

45. Faith in the God of the covenant gave rise to the understanding of the God of creation and of liberation. "I am the Lord your God who brought you out of Egypt and no other," would suggest this notion. However, creation precedes the covenant. It is worth noting here that the beliefs in the gods of fertility were quite common in the Middle Eastern religions and cultures. The Jewish belief in the God of creation is an antithesis of the belief in the gods of fertility in the non-Jewish world. The creation story was written while looking into the past actions of liberation by God.

46. Clobus, *Environmental Care*, 39.

the image and likeness of God. Therefore, the African narratives of justice, UMUMTU and ORUM, rightly portray the analogy of the interrelationship between creation and injustices, an approach lacking in Lebacqz's notion of justice.

In "Deeper Evangelization in the Third Millennium," the Catholic Bishops of the Association Member of Episcopal Conferences of Eastern Africa (AMECEA), emphasized the need to take a fresh look at evangelization in Africa. In their fourteenth plenary assembly, they maintained that deeper faith and action had been inadequate and that the need for a deeper evangelization is critical to the African church in the third millennium. Echoing the words of Paul VI in the apostolic exhortation, *Evangelii Nuntiandi* (*Evangelization in the Modern World*), the general assembly believed that deeper evangelization means evangelizing people's culture in a vital way, in depth and right to their roots.[47] However, the starting point is the human person in his or her relationship with others and with God:[48] "a deeper evangelization aims at the interior transformation of the world and its social, cultural, political and economical structures inspiring it with the values of the Kingdom of God."[49] Deeper evangelization involves, among other things, the clear proclamation of justice and peace.[50] Furthermore, the assembly stressed solidarity with the poor and respect for the integrity of God's creation.[51] The assembly further declared that the pastoral mandate of AMECEA is to promote human rights, justice and peace, freedom of religion, and to advocate for the oppressed and for good governance.[52]

Among the pastoral resolutions of the AMECEA as a prophetic voice on social justice and peace, the assembly directed that the Catholic social teachings should be compulsory in the AMECEA academic and pastoral institutions, including seminaries and houses of religious for-

---

47. "Deeper Evangelization," 264. Evangelization is a twofold process: identifying the positive elements and promoting them as well as discarding the negative elements. There are both positive and negative elements in every culture. Christ Jesus did not come to the world to abolish laws, traditions, or cultures. Rather he came to the world to fulfill them or perfect them.

48. Ibid., 265.

49. Ibid.

50. Ibid.

51. Ibid., 267.

52. Ibid., 269.

mation. The same teaching should be extended to "Christian political leaders, professionals, business people, the security personnel, forces and juridical institutions."[53] Basically, the assembly attempted to discuss the requirements of a deeper evangelization. Even if the assembly noted that the need for protecting our planet is part of integral justice, such a concept did not loom large in the assembly. Although the need for respect of God's creation is essential to a deeper evangelization, it is still vague in content, nevertheless. Here is the question: is respect for God's creation synonymous with protecting or conserving the creation? How does the protection of our planet earth fit in the program of deeper evangelization? As seen in the previous chapters, nature is integral to UMUMTU and ORUM. The understanding of these African cultural narratives offers a deeper understanding of justice and peace. Hence employing the image of UMUMTU and ORUM in constructing ecological and cosmic ethics is critical to a deeper evangelization in Africa.

The most definitive mention of ecological justice that the AMECEA gave was the following resolution:

> AMECEA, through its Justice and Peace desk, should develop and foster a spirituality of Justice and Peace that gives hope to victims of injustice. It has to create awareness on the demands of justice and peace, human rights, ecological issues and facilitate networking and collaboration with other Justice and Peace Commissions and other similar bodies and groups.[54]

There is no doubt that the above statement is one of the most important resolutions the bishops made. From this statement, however, it appears that ecology is not a justice and peace issue. Moreover, victims of injustice are exclusively referred to human victims, such as the poor, the marginalized, persons with disabilities, and the neglected.[55] In African religion, nature is integral to justice, unlike the bishops' notion of justice. Moreover, according to African cultural narrative of justice, victims of injustice include both humankind (the unborn, the living, and the living dead) and nature (animate and inanimate). Therefore, nature can be a victim of injustices if it is abused, threatened, or if it is deprived of due respect and protection. Hence, the African cultural narratives, UMUMTU

---

53. Ibid., 280–82.
54. Ibid.
55. Ibid., 281, nos. 58–59.

and ORUM, present a better notion of justice and peace than that of the bishops".

The assembly cautioned that a deeper evangelization is not a new program apart from what already exists in the gospel and in the living tradition. However, it stressed that deeper evangelization demands a new method: "Deeper evangelization is a new stage and a new method in the ongoing mission of announcing the Kingdom of God and making it penetrate in a deeper way both in the individual person and the human society."[56]

If deeper evangelization ought to consist of a new stage and a new method, then promoting greater justice and peace requires a new and a deeper understanding of justice and peace, which calls for a new method. Then, is the new method in place? The AMECEA Justice and Peace Desk, in collaboration with other justice and peace commissions, was entrusted with a task to develop and foster a spirituality of justice and peace by creating a new approach or a new method suitable to respond to the demands of deeper evangelization in the third millennium. Surprisingly, the assembly did not offer a description of the spirituality of justice and peace. To the best of my knowledge, I think that the AMECEA Justice and Peace Desk has not yet come up with a new method for a deeper evangelization. Neither contemporary theories of justice such as liberalism and libertarianism, nor others have provided for such a method. In the meantime, this study will attempt to create and to propose a method for promoting justice and peace in the third millennium. Such a method will become a necessary paradigm shift, which hopefully will offer inspiration or new insights for a fresh, vital, and deeper understanding of justice and peace in Africa and elsewhere.

This section examined the way the Catholic Church approached justice. In "Economic Justice for All" (1986), the U.S. Catholic Bishops argued for economic equality for all, as opposed to the American ethos that upholds the priority of civil and political rights over social and economic rights. The bishops maintained that human dignity or sacredness lived in community with others is the foundation of justice. Because liberal tradition restricts all justice to commutative justice, the bishops maintained that biblical justice interpreted as basic justice ought to consist of three major ingredients: commutative justice, distributive justice, and

---

56. Ibid., 264.

contributive justice. These dimensions of justice are critical to promoting the common good, such as economic justice for all. Although the bishops did hint at the importance of ecological justice, the subject did not loom large as an important factor in promoting economic justice for all. The bishops simply made a recommendation for the development of ecological ethics.

In "Justice in the World" (1971), the Synod of Bishops advocated for human development as a means to liberation from oppression. As with the U.S. Catholic Bishops, ecological justice did not loom large in this synod. The same observation can be made with respect to the AMECEA Bishops' "Deeper Evangelization" for its inadequate attention to ecological justice as a matter of urgency. AMECEA recommended a development of ecological ethics, at least. Searching for a paradigmatic theory of justice is ethically compelling and morally significant to implementing the church's recommendation for the need of ecological ethics.

8 Methodological Considerations for Constructing a Macrotheory of Justice

The exposition and critique of contemporary theories of justice was the task of part 1, in which their strengths and limitations were identified. As the task of part 2, a reinterpretation of justice was seen as critical to a deeper understanding of justice. The African cultural narratives of justice, UMUMTU, and the Jewish notion of justice, *sedaqah*, were employed in the search for a new understanding of justice. Common to both African religion and Jewish Scriptures is the factor of relationships in the understanding of justice. In African religion, the threads of justice extend not only to the spiritual domain of UMUMTU. Rather, justice encompasses the material-physical and temporal domains of UMUMTU. Consequently, the material-physical world is integral to UMUMTU, and it is therefore critical to a deeper understanding justice. Based on this understanding, justice is, therefore, interrelational, intrarelational, interdependent, and integral. UMUMTU is representative of a deeper understanding from which the principles of justice will be drawn. Constructing a framework for a deeper understanding of justice is the task of this section. To this effect, I adopt a relationship-centered ethical model or method, which the UMUMTU paradigm reflects.[1]

---

1. How is right from wrong determined? Or what is the method for determining right from wrong, and how is it obtained? Or how can the standards of ethics and morality develop? A number of methods have been developed in the areas of ethics in the course of years. These are deontology, teleology, virtue, consequentialism, such as utilitarianism, and so on. Catholic ethics and morality have shifted from one method to another. These shifts are commonly seen in the church's statements (papal, or Episcopal, and so on). Because of the church's stand on natural moral law, the method of deontology (adopted from Kant's ethical moral theory) is the common approach to Catholic ethics and morality: it is a moral duty to ensure that our actions or conduct conform to the natural moral law. However, there has been a shift from deontology to a relationship-responsibility ethical model as seen in the Vatican Council II, particularly in the document, *Gaudium et Spes* (also known as *The Church in the Modern World*), with its emphasis on the meaning and on the role of the human person as a moral subject in the modern world. For more information see Curran, *Catholic Social Teaching*, 80–81.

Because the role of the principles of justice is to guide, direct, govern, resolve, address, redress, order, or regulate relationships mediated by the exercising of rights and fulfilling of duties, benefits, and burdens, understanding justice is critical to understanding human rights and their correlative duties. The task here is to construct a framework from which the principles of deeper justice or macrojustice can be drawn. To this end, a number of the ingredients of the human rights model theory will be adopted, with a few modifications.[2] A wholesome theory of justice, reflective of UMUMTU (which promotes interrelationship, intrarelationship, interdependence, peace, happiness, harmony, order, community, solidarity, subsidiarity, integration), ought to address the following five fundamental threads: the bearer of justice, the object of justice, the nature of justice, the bearer of justice claims, and the basis of justice.

THE BEARER OF JUSTICE

The popular concept of justice as often understood as simply to "give what is due" is back in the spotlight once more. The question is, to whom is justice due and according to what principles or criteria? In other words, who is the moral claimant of justice? Is it the human person, the community, groups, or the general public? How is one entitled to justice, and what's the method for determining entitlement? Or what is the criterion of the entitlement of justice? For liberalism and libertarianism, the free and the rational human person is the beneficiary or the moral claimant of justice. For a utilitarian, it is the greatest number, and whereas for a communitarian, it is members in a human community. For a feminist, the bearer of justice is the human person as such, regardless of sex and gender.

In African religion, the moral claimant of justice is the greater whole, the community called UMUMTU or ORUM, unlike the free and the rational individual as in liberalism and in libertarianism or the human person associated with the human community as in communitarianism. It may be a little weird or strange to think that the cosmos, or *ulimwengu* is the bearer of justice. Strange as it may appear, *ulimwengu* is a crucial thread of justice in UMUMTU and ORUM, without which harmony, balance, order, happiness, development, and peace is almost impossible. Any disruption among those in the UMUMTU, i.e., nature, God, and humankind,

---

2. See "A Philosophical Assessment of the Interpretation of Human Rights in International Refugee Law and Public Policy" in Msoka, *Basic Human Rights*, 77–96.

leads to disorder in the universe. *Ulimwengu* or *oruka* is the habitat of the earthly life including that of humankind, plants, and animals, as well as the source of the human livelihood. Furthermore, *ulimwengu* is home of a variety of inanimate beings, which are the greatest source of energy and minerals that beautify and power our habitat. God, or *Mungu* or *Rua*, is the most important thread of justice in UMUMTU and ORUM.

Rob Clobus regrets that the notions of justice and peace have been exclusively referred to humankind. Clobus argues that justice, peace, and creation are intimately linked:

> Justice and Peace need each other as a mutual complement. Justice alone does not suffice. All by itself it is cool and efficient like tempered steel. It is clean and has no compassion. Peace is the enjoyment of the fruit of justice, extended to all people on earth. Peace needs Justice in order to bloom. Together Justice and Peace define humane living on earth. This union, beautiful though it is, is dangerously one sided. Although it reconciles humanity with its own kind and with God, it disregards creation. Such a disregard, as we know all too well, has perilously endangered the viability of the earth and so, in consequence, our own survival as a species.[3]

In what sense, therefore, is *Mungu* or *Rua* the subject of justice? What's the criterion for ascribing justice to *Mungu*? In African religion, *Mungu* is believed to be the Creator, Giver, Source, and Sustainer of *mtu* and *ulimwengu*.[4] The relationship with *Mungu* is critical to the survival or the sustenance of *mtu* and *ulimwengu*. Therefore, *Mungu* is the subject of justice par excellence.

In "Economic Justice for All," for example, the three dimensions of basic justice (commutative, distributive, and contributive) were seen as critical to a life of dignity. However, the relationship of humankind with the planet earth, the source of our livelihood, did not loom large in the pastoral letter.[5] In "Deeper Evangelization in the Third Millennium," ecological issues were seen as separate from justice and peace.[6] In African religion, not only is humankind sacred but nature or *ulimwengu* is also sacred, and therefore it is integral part of the community, UMUMTU. Hence, the right understanding of *ulimwengu* and *oruka* is integral to

3. Clobus, *Environmental Care*, 65–66.
4. Refer to *African Cultural Narratives of Justice*, chapter 5 of this book.
5. U.S. Catholic Bishops, "Economic Justice for All," 595, nos. 68–70.
6. "Deeper Evangelization," 281, no. 58.

deeper justice and peace. Therefore, Christian social ethics enriched by African cultural narratives of UMUMTU and ORUM offers a deeper understanding that humankind, nature, and God are the bearers of justice.[7]

THE OBJECT OF JUSTICE

From the perspective of UMUMTU, it was established that the claimants of justice are humankind, nature, and God. The question is: what goods ought the claimant of justice to enjoy, assert, or enforce? Or what are the claims of justice? What claims does UMUMTU demand? What claims of justice does God, *Mungu*, or *Rua* demand? For a liberal, the claimant of justice demands fairness in choosing the principles of justice behind the veil of ignorance. Most importantly, the claimant of justice demands equal civil and political rights (negative). For a libertarian, the claimant of justice demands just entitlements or goods according to the historical method. For a utilitarian, the claimant of justice demands actions or rules that contribute to the greatest happiness. For a feminist, the claimant of justice demands equal treatment of individuals regardless of sex and gender. For a communitarian, the claimant of justice demands the allocation or distribution of goods according to shared social understandings of these goods.

Biblical justice regards the human person as the claimant of justice in enjoying equal treatment according to equal human dignity. For UMUMTU and ORUM, the claimant of justice demands equal protection or enjoyment of the abundant life, which results in peace, harmony, balance, fulfillment, happiness, equilibrium, wholeness, integration, community, solidarity, and subsidiarity. Enjoyment of abundant life is an expression of God's justice in the world. Based on the wholesome notion of justice, Christian social ethics enriched by African social cultural narratives of UMUMTU and ORUM offers a deeper understanding of the object of justice.

THE NATURE OF JUSTICE

The nature of justice deals with legitimate moral claims for certain goods, which command for a higher priority in satisfying them. This is the ques-

---

7. Ibid., 233–34. The call to enrich our Christian faith with African cultural values is perfectly in line with the AMECEA Bishops' call for the inculturated ways of evangelization.

tion the nature of justice will answer: What goods command the highest priority in the conflict of claims?

The main focus of liberalism is fairness in choosing the principles of justice behind the veil of ignorance. *Individual equality* in enjoying civil and political rights (negative) overrides enjoying socioeconomic rights (positive). Therefore, justice regards negative civil and political rights as the highest priority. However, liberalism proposes a social scheme by which some level of economic rights are offered to protect the least advantaged through the difference principle.

For a libertarian, the nature of justice is basically commutative. This means *individual liberty* (negative)—the ability to make free choices in acquiring the goods and in exchanging them with anyone of one's choice—enjoys the highest priority. Disadvantaged persons have no chance to survive in this system of justice. The libertarian system leaves room for charity simply as a philanthropic venture and not as a morally binding obligation.

For a utilitarian, actions that promote the *greatest happiness* or which mitigate pain enjoy the highest priority. Mill believes that the suffering caused by poverty and diseases can be reduced to minimum limits through the progress of science. Mill, however, remains unclear how the greatest happiness trickles down to individuals, particularly the disadvantaged.

For a communitarian, *membership* is the highest distributive good. Allocation or transfer of goods to members who possess the shared understanding of these goods enjoys the highest priority. There is a small provision in this system of justice for protecting the nonmembers by including them through the principle of mutual aid.

For a feminist, justice focuses on promoting the *social equality of women* as the highest priority.

From a Christian perspective, actions or structures that contribute to the promotion and to the protection of *human dignity*, particularly of the poor, the voiceless, the marginalized, and vulnerable, ought to enjoy the highest priority.

From the perspective of African religion, justice, UMUMTU and ORUM, is proactive, and it is determined by the way the relationships of God, humankind, and nature are ordered to promote the abundant life and dignity. According to UMUMTU and ORUM, actions or structures that contribute to the promotion of abundant life and dignity in both the human and the nonhuman community ought to enjoy the highest priority. Christian social ethics enriched by African justice, UMUMTU, offers a macro-understanding of the nature of justice.

THE RESPONDENTS OF JUSTICE CLAIMS

Justice is a claim, which demands for an appropriate moral and legal response. Justice claims generate four fundamental correlative duties. These include the duty to avoid depriving justice (negative), the duty to protect others from depriving justice (positive), the duty to aid or assist those deprived of justice (positive), and the duty to redress injustices and to restore justice (positive).

The Duty to Refrain from Depriving Justice

The duty to avoid from depriving justice (negative) enjoys the highest priority over the positive duties as a characteristic of the liberal and libertarian tradition. There is no doubt that actions, laws, or structures that threaten or violate right relationships or right conduct should be avoided. Nevertheless, ways and means have to be in place in order to fulfill such duties. According to the liberal and libertarian tradition, the negative conception of justice as freedom from interference is the highest priority, compared to positive justice, conceived as freedom for relationships. However, an effective negative justice requires the existence of positive action or social arrangements and legal guarantees.

The Christian duties of justice require not only a negative action (negative freedom) but they also require a positive action (positive freedom) by both individuals and social institutions. The duty to refrain from depriving someone the right relationships with God, humankind, and nature requires not only a negative action, but also a positive action. According to African religion, the wholesome justice, UMUMTU and ORUM, offers the possibility of extending both the negative and positive duties of justice towards humankind and nature as an expression of God's justice in the universe, unlike the liberal and libertarian tradition. Hence, Christian social ethics enriched by African cultural narratives, UMUMTU and ORUM, offers a deeper understanding that satisfying positive and negative justice towards humankind and nature requires both negative and positive duties of justice.

The Duty to Protect Others from Deprivations of Justice

Satisfying the duty of justice to refrain from depriving justice is critical to the satisfaction of the other duties of justice. If the duties to avoid depriving justice are fully satisfied, then the duties to protect from deprivations of justice seem unnecessary. However, it is not always the case in this imperfect world. Failure to avoid depriving justice (negative) provides the ground for satisfying the duty of protecting others from the deprivation of justice (positive).

As a libertarian, Nozick maintains that the minimal state is justified in order to allow everyone enjoy individual freedom. He also maintains that a more extensive state violates the freedom of choice. When great need arises or situation requires, the government can intervene in the lives of individuals in the interest of maintaining national security by preserving territorial integrity and sovereignty. Furthermore, a government's actions are justified when the individual right to property is at stake as well as when the holdings in question are not historical. The principle of the rectification of injustices is invoked here to justify the state's intervention.

The liberal tradition offers some protection for the least advantaged in society. Rawls believes that justice is not only about fairness in choosing the principles of justice behind the veil of ignorance. It is also about redressing extreme inequalities by having in place social arrangements to maximize benefits for the least advantaged.

Walzer's theory of justice is basically a defense of equality and pluralism. The principle of complex equality, which Walzer proposes, as opposed to simple equality, is intended to justify inequalities within the same spheres of distributions. Walzer believes that the principle will eliminate monopoly, domination, and tyranny in society. This approach to justice challenges feminists' advocacy for simple equality between the sexes. Membership in community is the criterion for enjoying social goods. However, Walzer believes that strangers across common borders ought to be offered some protection through the principle of mutual aid to avoid injustices of domination and tyranny by members of the community.

In African religion, promoting the right relationship among God, humankind, and nature is central to UMUMTU and ORUM. This notion of justice is becoming more and more relevant today when weapon proliferations are threatening the very existence of humankind and of nature. Therefore, Christian social ethics enriched by the African cultural narratives of UMUMTU and ORUM offers a deeper understanding of the duties to protect humankind and nature as an expression of God's justice in the universe.

The Duty to Assist or Aid Those Deprived of Justice

The duty to assist those deprived of justice is a result of the failure to refrain from depriving justice and of the failure to protect others from deprivations of justice. The question here is: who is the bearer of such duties of justice in this case? If individuals or groups fail in their duties to refrain from depriving justice, then some kind of social arrangement ought to be in place. In this case, one can say that public institutions, like the government, ought to intervene to protect those deprived of justice. If the government fails in its duties to refrain from actions causing deprivations of justice, or if the government is the perpetrator of injustices, then the government ought to be brought into account through a legal system to assist those deprived. For this measure to succeed, the government's institutions such as the legislature and judiciary ought to work interdependently. Similarly, if the government fails in its duties to protect from deprivations, then some kind of social arrangements have to be deployed to assist those deprived of justice.

Here is the worst-case scenario: actions or the inaction of governments cause people to flee their homeland and seek asylum in another country. Walzer argues that through the principle of justice of mutual aid, strangers or nonmembers within common borders should be assisted by being admitted into the society to avoid domination and tyranny by its members. To succeed, the inclusion of nonmembers into society may involve both domestic and international intervention.[8] Neither Rawls nor Nozick offers such provisions in their treatment of justice.

For Christians, love of neighbor is a duty of justice and an expression of God's love and justice such that those deprived of justice must receive assistance as a preferential treatment. In African religion, not only is humankind the bearer of justice, but nature is as well. The African expression, "Whatever falls on one falls on all" supports that proposition. Thus, satisfying the duties to assist those deprived of justice such as nature and humankind is equal to fulfilling duties toward God. Anything less would lead to a rupture of justice of the community, UMUMTU and ORUM.

---

8. See Msoka, *Basic Human Rights*, 102, 162–67.

Fulfilling the duties of assisting humankind and nature deprived of justice brings about the restoration of justice in the universe, in the short-term. Redressing injustices, however, brings into a complete circle the moral duty of restoring justice in the long-term. Therefore, Christian social ethics enriched by the African cultural narratives UMUMTU and ORUM offer a deeper understanding of the fact that assistance ought to be offered to humankind and nature to restore the wholeness and the integrity of creation.

The Duty to Redress Injustices

The duties of justice not only demand that those deprived of justice be assisted in the short-term but they also demand the redressing of injustices, which is paramount for the restoration of justice in the universe in the long-term. Redressing injustices aims at restoring, reestablishing, or putting back on track relationships that are ruptured, tainted, wrong, or inappropriate. Often, the legal system is largely aimed at rectifying broken human relationships or redressing the wrong done against humans and thus restoring justice in human society. The African cultural narratives of justice, UMUMTU and ORUM, go further than just dealing with human relationships; they include nonhuman relationships. Because nature is the bearer of justice, any act of injustice committed against nature poses an ethical problem to peace and harmony in the universe. Based on this proposition, it follows that any act of injustice against nature demands redress. This means that any human actions that have negatively impacted nature ought to be redressed.

Redressing injustices has to move from intrarelationships to interrelationships. Because UMUMTU or ORUM is a macrointegral whole, any disruption of the right relationship within humankind (intrajustice) has a negative impact upon nature and the universe as a whole (interjustice). Hence, redressing intra-injustice or intrinsic injustice is the starting point for the restoration of interjustice or extrinsic justice in the universe. Restoration of intrajustice is the condition sine qua non for the restoration of interjustice. Because justice is grounded in God, having in place the right relationship with God is a precondition for the restoration of intrajustice and interjustice. It also follows that acts of justice for humankind and nature are considered an expression of God's justice in the universe.

The concepts of intrajustice and interjustice can also be seen in the sin of Adam and Eve. As seen earlier, from the perspective of the biblical theme of creation, the rupture of justice started with the fall of Adam and Eve in the garden of Eden. The rebellion against God's law of love started from the inside out (intrajustice): a deliberate decision to be totally free from the law of God and be free for the created things at the exclusion of God. Consequently, the creature was turned into a god, and God was turned into a creature. This scenario was a perfect expression of idolatry.

The lack of respect for the nature of humankind and the nature of the cosmos provides a basis for an inproper relationship between humankind and the cosmos. Respecting humankind and nature is the beginning of redressing injustices.[9] Then, the recognition of injustices is the second stage of redressing injustices,[10] followed by repentance, renunciation, remorse, and reparations.[11] Redressing injustices by reparations is perhaps the way most people think justice ought to be served. Giving to one what is due implies compensations for the wrong done, as Lebacqz notes:

> But reparation means repairing, mending, or restoring to a proper state. It means making amends or compensation for a wrong or injury done. It is therefore the proper response from the perpetrator of injustice to the victim of that injustice. If one genuinely takes responsibility for wrongs done, then surely the response in justice is to attempt to set right those wrongs. Without reparations or some attempt at redressing, it is questionable whether responsibility has really been taken.[12]

Mending intrarelationships (UMUMTU) is critical to the restoration of justice in the universe and achieving external justice or interjustice. According to Nozick, injustices result when the holdings in acquisition and the holdings in exchange are not historical. Making people accountable for their wrongdoing is the responsibility of the state.[13] According to Mill, it is just for a person to enjoy a right or a good or undergo an evil

---

9. The model for redressing injustices was inspired by Lebacqz, *Justice in an Unjust World*, 104. According to Lebacqz, addressing injustices has been restricted to human relationships. In my study, redressing injustices includes both humans and nature.

10. Ibid., 108.

11. Ibid., 111–20.

12. Ibid., 117.

13. See *Justice and Libertarianism*, chapter 3 of this book.

when it is deserved and unjust when it is the reverse.[14] Sacred Scriptures consider justice as freedom from sin and its structures to freedom for God and for each other.[15] In African religion, the chief goal of redressing injustices is not simply to impose punishment or retribution on the wrongdoer. Rather, redressing injustices is aimed at bringing about reconciliation between the perpetrator and the victim in a particular community, for whatever falls on one, falls to all.[16]

Restorative justice should be preceded by corrective justice and retributive justice. Nozick's principle of rectification of injustice applies in those cases where the holdings in acquisitions did not follow the historical method. This principle redresses the acts of injustices against the human victims and not the victims of nature. Because in African religion humankind and nature are the bearers of justice, they are also considered the victims of injustices. To summarize, Christian social ethics enriched by the African cultural narratives of UMUMTU and ORUM offers a deeper understanding that redressing the acts of injustices against humankind (intrainjustice) and Nature (interjustice) leads to the restoration of God's justice in the universe.

THE BASIS OF JUSTICE

The basis of justice answers the question, what's the ultimate foundation of justice? Here is a partial summary of part 1: Nozick maintains that every person has the right to life and the liberty to private property. The human person ought to be treated not as an object, but rather as a subject. Nozick believes that holdings are just if they are historical. This means that one has what one has through the acquisitions of unowned property or through free exchange. Hence, the basis of justice is entitlements procured historically. Furthermore, Nozick does not consider justice in terms of redistribution; however, he provides room for redistribution through philanthropic charity not as a morally binding obligation, but rather as a personal initiative of free choice. Otherwise, making it a moral obligation would violate the individual's right to freedom of choice.

Rawls maintains that justice is fairness: that the principles of justice have to be chosen behind the veil of ignorance by equal free and rational

14. See *Justice and Utilitarianism*, chapter 2 of this book.
15. See *Biblical Narratives of Justice*, chapter 6 of this book.
16. See *African Cultural Narratives of Justice*, chapter 5 of this book.

persons. The basis of justice is the equality of the individual in choosing the principles of justice. In real life, however, equality applies only to the first principle of justice: civil and political liberties (freedom from). The principle of social and economic rights does not apply to all in equal terms. To Rawls, admitting some inequalities is not in any way unethical and immoral. Inequalities are justified in so far as the benefits are maximized for the good of the least advantaged through the difference principle (freedom for). Rawls does not offer an ultimate basis for the equality of the individual in general or for the protection of the least advantaged individuals in particular.

Walzer believes that the principle of complex equality would eliminate monopoly, domination, and tyranny. To avoid a community's domination over strangers, the latter ought to be accepted or included into the political community through the principle of mutual aid. The question is: what is the justification of the principle of mutual aid? Why should strangers such as immigrants or refugees be accorded protection such as hospitality, shelter, sanctuary, or citizenship? Walzer is unable to provide the ultimate justification for the immorality of monopoly, domination, and tyranny.

The ethical paradigmatic theory of justice, UMUMTU, offers a thick, or macro-description of justice by focusing on humankind, nature, and God as the bearers of justice. What is the foundation for such a claim that nature, man, and God are the bearers of justice? Or what is the basis for claiming that the abundant life is the object of justice? Or what is the grounding principle(s) for assisting those deprived of justice? Or what is the basis for redressing injustices and restoring justice? Answering these fundamental questions paves the way to establishing the basis for refraining, protecting, assisting, redressing and restoring justice in the universe.

According to African religion, the basis of justice is grounded in anthropology and cosmology.[17] In African religion, humankind is sacred because of the sacred character of UMUMTU in which *Mungu*, *Rua*, or God is considered the giver and sustainer of life.[18] In contrast, the Catholic

---

17. The Catholic Church's social teaching is grounded in two anthropological principles: the sacredness or dignity of the human person and the social character of the human person. Hence, these two principles are the bedrock of justice. In African religion, justice is grounded both in anthropology and cosmology, as illustrated by the UMUMTU paradigm of relationships.

18. See *African Cultural Narratives of Justice*, chapter 5 in this book.

Church's social teaching is grounded in two fundamental anthropological principles: the sacredness or dignity and the social character of the human person. The biblical tradition, which inspires the church's social doctrine, brings to full light the nature of the human person as sacred because humans share in God's image and likeness.[19] The image and likeness, which links humanity to the abundant life, was diminished by the sin of Adam and Eve and led to personal and social disorder. The sin of Adam and Eve signified the refusal to faithfully live out the relationship with God, the source of the abundant life. The relationship, which leads to abundant life but was affected by sin, has been restored by Christ's redemption through the new covenant of love, justice, and peace. Therefore, assisting those deprived of justice is a sacred duty of love and not simply a philanthropic venture as Nozick claims. Implementing the principle of mutual aid would assist those in need. However, Walzer falls short of providing the ultimate basis for such an endeavor. Rawls's justification of inequalities in exercising the social and economic rights to maximize the benefits for the least advantaged through the difference principle also lacks a solid basis. UMUMTU and the Bible will provide a basis of such protection for the least advantaged individuals. African religion goes even further than the Bible does in providing the basis for protecting both humankind and nature.

In African religion, the cosmos is sacred because of the sacred characteristic of UMUMTU. This belief entails sacred duties towards nature as an expression of the social characteristics of humankind. The earth is given to the whole of humanity as a gratuitous gift, and all human beings possess an equal claim to it and the resources it offers. Actions of greed or misuse of natural resources are a violation of the sacred character of UMUMTU. It has been commonly held or thought that humankind is the only creature made in God's image and likeness, resulting in the lack of an adequate respect of nature by humankind. Because all creation, both humanity and nature, is made by God, everything bears the mark of the creator. Rob Clobus argues:

> As the Book of Genesis refers to human beings as having been made in the image of God, can we rightly proclaim that no other creatures of the earth have been thus made? We are differentiated

---

19. The argument for the theological justification of human rights is the same argument employed for the basis of justice. For detailed information see Msoka, *Basic Human Rights*, 110–12.

from the rest of creation in that we alone are reflective and can act upon our conclusions. Nonetheless all creatures are truly God's handiwork.[20]

The social characteristics of humankind do not only apply to the right relationship between one person and another. It also applies to the right relationship between humankind and nature. It is worth noting here that the common understanding of the social character of humankind is basically applied to human relationships in most of the Catholic Church's documents, whereas the pragmatic justice enacted through UMUMTU applies to relationships between humans, the cosmos, and the creator. The former applies to both humankind and the natural world, thus making it the most robust macrotheory of justice ever.

The right relationship between humankind and nature mirrors the relationship of humans with Christ, the justice of God. Solidarity between humankind, nature, and God through Christ's work of redemption brings about abundant life in the universe. The experience of abundant life starts from the inside (intrajustice) out (interjustice), resulting in wholesome peace in the universe. Deeper evangelization in Africa, as the theme of the AMECEA bishops stands, requires doing justice in its entirety, namely to the whole of creation, humankind and nature.

THE RETRIEVAL OF THE JUSTICE PRINCIPLES

So far, by studying both biblical narratives of justice, *sedaqah/dikaiosyne*, and African cultural narratives of justice, UMUMTU or ORUM, five fundamental threads for a macrotheory of justice have already been identified. Based on the analysis of these fundamental threads, the fourfold principles of justice will be retrieved as the framework for the construction of a macrojustice theory:

Principle 1: Ethical and moral recognition that humankind, nature, and God are the bearers of justice.

Principle 2: Ethical and moral recognition that the abundant life (peace, harmony, integrity, equilibrium, wellness, happiness, wholeness, and so on) is the fundamental good or fruit of justice.

Principle 3: Ethical and moral imperative that the duty to assist those deprived of justice is an expression of solidarity of love for the victims

---

20. Clobus, *Environmental Care*, 38–39.

of injustice and thus that it ought to enjoy the highest priority in public policy (distributive justice).

Principle 4: Ethical and moral imperative that perpetrators of injustice ought to bear the moral responsibility of redressing and restoring injustices (legal/contributive justice).

A REALITY CHECK

Through the study of the African cultural narratives of justice, UMUMTU and ORUM, four major principles of justice have been retrieved as a basis for peace in Africa and for the rest of the world. However, if UMUMTU and ORUM is a homegrown model of justice and thus so relevant in promoting the culture of life or the abundant life as opposed to the culture of death as demonstrated by social conflicts, refugee influx, civil strife, violence, corruption, political instability, and economic stagnation, what went wrong with some parts of Africa? For example, the 1994 Rwandan genocide, the failed state of Somalia, the western Darfur conflict in Sudan, the displacement of the civilian populations and hundreds of thousands of deaths, rapes, and so on, in the Democratic Republic of the Congo,[21] and the 2008 sociopolitical crises in Kenya and Zimbabwe are some of the worst-case scenarios of social disorder and the loss of life and property. Again, there is a similar question or concern: what went wrong with America, with its declaration of being "one nation under God"? The American nation founded by those people who fled from religious persecution in Europe has been shaped by various cultural narratives over the years. These include the biblical story of the covenant; the story of success and the self-made man and woman; the story of well-being, self-realization, and self-worth; and finally the story of the mission of America as a leader in the world.[22]

What are cultural narratives? In *Social Ethics: An Examination of American Moral Traditions*, Roger G. Betsworth describes the meaning of cultural narratives as follows:

> Cultural narratives differ from ordinary stories told in a culture. In order to be told, a story must be set within a culture. The cultural narrative establishes the world in which an ordinary story makes

---

21. For an in-depth analysis of the root causes of the humanitarian crises in sub-Saharan Africa, see Msoka, *Basic Human Rights*, chap. 1.

22. Betsworth, *Social Ethics*, 16–18.

> sense. It informs people's sense of the story in which they set the story of their own lives. The history, scriptures, and literary narratives of a culture, the stories told of and in family and clan, and the stories of popular culture all articulate and clarify the world of the cultural narrative in which they are set. Thus a cultural narrative is not directly told.[23]

Cultural narratives are languages, stories, proverbs, or metaphors that make sense of our selves and of the world. What's this sense? Or what's the ethical and moral content of cultural narratives? Rogers explains, "Because they fashion a world, cultural narratives establish those distinctions between right and wrong actions that direct the self outward toward communal purposes in which alone the self can be realized."[24]

The biblical story of the covenant is more relevant in this case than the other stories. The story was built upon the belief that human actions ought to be judged in light of the covenantal relationship: I will be your God and you will be my people. In light of the new covenant, the formation of the new people is through Christ, and as a response to this covenant, the love for God and love for neighbor are moral imperatives.[25] Is it not awkward to think that those oppressed in Europe became the oppressor in America? The newcomers launched an assault upon the Native Americans and their land. Their fundamental rights to life, liberty, and property were violated. Conflicts of interest that led to wars caused many of Native Americans lose their lives, become displaced and homeless in their own homeland, or be pushed to the reservations or hostile areas. These brutal events altered in the most fundamental ways the history of a people. Conflict of interests was sorely to blame for the injustices committed upon these indigenous populations, their land, and their religious beliefs. In the aftermath of these events, the newcomers lost their sense of the covenant and its demands regarding the treatment of others, as stipulated in the cultural narrative of the covenant. As time went by, the biblical story of the covenant was overshadowed by new emerging cultural narratives that continued to shape the cultural life of America. The darkest moments in the history of America were characterized by the evils of slavery, wars against the Native Americans, civil war, and the

---

23. Ibid., 15.
24. Ibid.
25. Ibid., 16.

assault on civil rights within an independent nation. Are these darkest moments far from over?

From these scenarios, one can now understand the reasons why there have been such dark moments in the history of Africa, despite the existence of the African cultural narratives of justice, UMUMTU. Africa lost its sense of the moral values of UMUMTU just as Americans lost the sense of the moral values of the biblical story of the covenant. The loss of UMUMTU has been due not only to internal interventions like tribal conflicts, clashes, or wars. The loss of the moral values of UMUMTU was, to a large extent, due to foreign interventions such as slavery; the scramble for African resources, land, and labor and the partition of Africa; colonialism; neocolonialism; foreign religions (which ignore the cultural and moral values of African religion); cold war politics and conflicts; post–cold war conflicts; liberal democracy; and so on.

First, slavery was the gravest evil against a people and their history. By this act, people were uprooted from their ancestral land. This means that justice had been ruptured, namely their relationships with each other (because families, clans, and tribes were torn apart), with their ancestral land, and with their traditional religious beliefs were broken.

Second, the 1884 Berlin Conference embarked upon the scramble for and partition of Africa that sliced the continent into shares held by different European imperialists like the French, the British, the German, the Portuguese, the Spanish, and so on. The borders were drawn up without any consideration for the sociological composition of the populations. Consequently, common ancestral land was violated, and communities were split down the middle. Foreign intervention, like colonialism, significantly impacted their common language, art, heritage, social cohesion, cultural moral traditions, and religion.[26]

Third, the cold war in the 1970s and 1990s made Africa a battleground for ideological and military competition between the Eastern Block and the Western Block. As a result of these conflicts, many lost their lives, communities were dismembered, and hundreds of thousands were displaced, or became homeless, or refugees.[27]

Fourth, some missionaries considered African religion as barbaric and superstitious. Therefore, African religion, mistakenly thought to

---

26. Msoka, *Basic Human Rights*, 7–14, 19–21.
27. Ibid., 21–26.

be animism (worship of spirits), was considered incompatible with Christianity. Because Christianity never took root in the African way of life, Africans lived a double life: Christian life in the day and African life in the night. The African worldview was significantly disrupted; their relationships with each other, with nature, and with God were weakened. Consequently, Africans lost their sense of wholeness, wholesomeness, unity of life, solidarity, and peace.

Fifth, modern political changes that swept Africa in the early 1960s did not spare the continent from social disruption. Historically, a sense of community and an emphasis on group rights has characterized African societies. Liberalism, on the other hand, focuses more on individual rights than on people's rights. Liberal democracy that has been introduced in Africa as a model political system has not been successful in many countries due to its conflict with the African worldview.[28]

These factors and others contributed to the erosion of the African social fabric. A rediscovery of the African cultural narratives, UMUMTU and ORUM, is critical to restoring the holistic justice and peace in the continent. The four principles drawn from the macrotheory of justice, UMUMTU and ORUM, ought to be the basis for restoring justice and peace. The imagery of UMUMTU and ORUM is not only relevant to Africa; it is also relevant to global justice and peace. Because of the cosmocentric character of human interrelationships, justice or injustice committed in one place may affect another place. Globalization is a good example.

THE ETHICAL AND MORAL RAMIFICATIONS OF THE NEW PRINCIPLES OF JUSTICE

The recognition that humankind, nature, and God are the bearers of justice is quite significant in dealing with the violation of the right conduct or relationship among people and between humanity and nature. Because of the intimate connection that exists in UMUMTU (intrajustice), any violation of dignity against humankind and nature is a violation against God's justice in the universe (interjustice). Violations of intrajustice have an impact on the world justice and peace (interjustice). Hence, any public policy that enhances these relationships ought to be promoted, and that

---

28. UMUMTU is equivalent to cosmotheandrism. See Msoka, "Cosmotheandrization of Human Rights," 62–92.

which does the opposite ought to be discouraged. Exercising this principle would resolve conflicts between individuals or groups and between individuals and nature.

Recognition that the abundant life is the fundamental fruit or good of justice is quite significant, not only in dealing with intrapeace within humankind and within nature, but also in dealing with world peace (interjustice). Often, peace is understood as the absence of war or conflict (negative) between individuals, groups, states, or nations. UMUMTU, on the other hand, portrays wholesome peace or shalom (positive). Because peace is a sum total of all that makes humankind and nature whole, any actions that violate intrapeace violate interpeace. This proposition implies that local decisions or policies that promote the abundant life can have an impact on the rest of the world. Likewise, anything contrary has an adverse effect on the rest of the world. For instance, decisions made in Washington, DC or Brussels have an impact elsewhere such as in Tanzania, Bolivia, Cuba, Venezuela, Iraq, and so on. Wars in the Middle East have a negative impact on the world oil market prices and the cost of living in China, India, Africa, and so on. Hurricanes in the Gulf of Mexico of the United States have a negative impact on the oil prices and other consumer commodities locally and globally.

It is important to note that the positive and negative demands of justice are critical for promoting the abundant life. Often the weak, the poor, the voiceless, and the vulnerable are deprived of abundant life. Even if consumer products are important, toxic materials from industrialized nations destroy land and marine food sources by polluting rivers, lakes, oceans, and so on. People can become victims of an unregulated financial system in the global economy, which is what occurred during the collapse of the financial banks and the mortgage housing industry in the United States and elsewhere in 2008. Who is going to defend or protect those who have lost their jobs, savings, or investments? It is assumed that the bailing out of the financial banks by the U.S. federal government allowed the chief executives to continue to enjoy life from their huge salaries and benefits without being held accountable for their actions. And who will defend the victims of political violence in Kenya (2007) or in Zimbabwe (2008)? Some kind of social arrangements should be made to assist those deprived of abundant life. Assisting those deprived of the abundant life ought to be the highest priority in public policy.

It is an ethical and moral imperative that the perpetration of injustices against humankind and nature be considered a violation of God's justice in the universe. It ought to be a priority of public policy that the victims of injustices, including nature, will be accorded preferential treatment. It is often thought that the victims of injustices are exclusively humans. According to UMUMTU, however, nature can also be a victim of injustices. Which one, then, enjoys the priority when it comes to assisting or protecting from injustices? One would think that assisting the human victims of injustices is the first priority because according to the priestly creation story, humanity is considered the pinnacle of God's creation (Gen 1:1–3)[29] and the primary beneficiary of God's love. Following this order in creation, protecting nature becomes the second priority. As seen earlier, nature can be a victim of injustices or abuses by humankind. Secularism contributes greatly to the desacralization of nature. Because nature is sacred, the abuse of it results in a morally disorderly act or sin and consequently results in cosmic disorder.

Sin, therefore, bears both anthropological and cosmic characters. The cosmic character of sin is often ignored by public policy makers as insignificant. Furthermore, Catholic theology has paid too little attention to the organic development of cosmological ethics.[30] The study of macrojustice contributes to the understanding of the necessary link between ethics and humankind and between ethics and nature. The theocentric understanding of humankind and nature provides the justification for such a link. This kind of understanding can lead to protecting and promoting the abundant life, a notion lacking in the contemporary theories of justice.[31]

Restoring God's justice in the world requires redressing injustices against humankind and nature. The perpetrators of injustices against hu-

---

29. Clobus, *Environmental Care*, 35–36.

30. The use of the term "cosmology" instead of "ecology" seems to fit better in the study of *umumtulogy* of justice. Ecology is the study of the environment, i.e., what surrounds humankind, for example, air, water, plants, and so on. Cosmology is the study of the physical nature or cosmos and is not simply about what surrounds humankind. Hence, cosmology is more an appropriate notion than ecology. The use of ecological ethics is rampart in Catholic pastoral letters and in public policy documents. The use of cosmological ethics fits better in the study of an umumtulogy of justice.

31. The interconnection of positive and negative justice is lacking in liberalism and libertarianism. See *Justice and Liberalism*, chapter 1, and *Justice and Libertarianism*, chapter 3 of part 1 of this book.

manity and nature ought to bear the moral responsibility for redressing injustices in the world. Moral responsibility includes satisfying the duties of retributive justice or corrective and reparatory justice, such as undergoing punishment or paying compensation.

Restoration of justice leads to abundant life. A rediscovery of a new theory of justice will bring a great deal of hope to thousands of victims of injustices, including people displaced by both the natural disasters as well as man-made disasters across the world. Christian social ethics enriched by African cultural narratives, UMUMTU and ORUM, offers a constructive macrotheory of justice for the restoration of abundant life.

Pius M. Ssentumbwe presents a forceful argument for building a peaceful world. Ssentumbwe maintains that a peaceful world requires environmental protection:

> Creation must be given a voice, present generations and those to come. We must listen to the people who fish the sea, harvest the forest, till the soil and mine the earth, as well as to those who advance the conservation, protection and preservation of the environment.[32]

While it is critical to listen to those people such as fishermen and others, it is, however, extremely important to listen to nature as well.[33] It is often thought that powerlessness or voicelessness is reserved to the human victims of injustices. Is nature, a victim of injustices, silent or voiceless? Does it speak a language? Is nature defenseless and vulnerable? What happens if the ecosystems in nature are distorted or disturbed by humans? What might be nature's reaction or response to abuses? History has shown that nature reacts against injustices when the right relationships between humankind and nature's systems are either ignored, disturbed, or distorted by humans. It is almost a consensus that the rising temperatures, rising sea levels, and the flooding experienced around the globe have been caused, to some extent, by global warming. Nature

---

32. Ssentumbwe, "Peace," 213.

33. Schonborn, *Chance or Purpose*, 150–52. Schonborn argues that creation speaks to individuals through its language, its rhythms, its meaning, and its logic. He continues to argue that creation speaks to people about responsibility for creation. I may add that, throughout this study, I have emphasized that often we are forced to listen to the voice of nature when disasters strike due to irresponsible human activity in the world. Maintaining a good balance between science, development, and the protection of nature is critical to preventing catastrophes, poverty, chaos, and deaths in the universe.

speaks volumes by reacting violently or speaking angrily, so to say, against injustices committed by humankind's actions, so much so that catastrophes and death have been the outcome, unfortunately. To restore cosmic justice, each one of us has the moral responsibility to listen to the cries of nature with both ears widely open and act appropriately. Failure to listen carefully and act promptly and appropriately can result in chaos.

Nature as much as humankind calls for liberation from injustices inflicted upon it. Clobus concurs with this proposition:

> The neglect of the whole earth as being in need of liberation was apparent in the action programmes of social justice and peace groups of the recent past. Their almost exclusive concentration on people who are oppressed and exploited by their fellow human beings overlooked the fact that the whole earth is in need of liberation and that a new society and a just world can only take root once we recognize our human dependence on the earth, recognize the rights of all life, and develop a way of life which is friendly to all. The inclusion of the notion of Integrity of Creation in the Justice and Peace concept has enhanced our humane Christian concern to such an extent that it now has the added dimension it needs in order to be relevant to the whole of creation.[34]

Reconciliation implies liberation from injustices against humankind and nature, and thus the restoration of the right relationship between humankind and nature becomes possible. Because humans are the major agents committing injustices against nature, humankind ought to be part of the solution in redressing such injustices. Liberation means human freedom from personal and cosmic sin to the restoration of abundant life. Liberation also means restoring the right relationship between humankind and nature.

Rectification of injustices does not only apply to the restoration of good human relationships (agreements, contracts, or business transactions) as Nozick has shown. Rather, according to UMUMTU, rectification of injustices is aimed at restoring the right relationship to both humankind and nature. Walzer's notion of complex equality may apply here analogously: humankind and nature belong to different spheres of existence in such a way that each of these is an entity by its own right. For example,

---

34. Clobus, *Environmental Care*, 66. By *creation*, Clobus refers mainly to that which has life, such as plants and animals. In African religion, *nature* refers to both the animate and inanimate creation.

if humans cross over into the sphere of nature without taking into an account the principle of inner logic (the intrinsic connection between them) or without respecting the right of autonomy of each sphere, such an action is, in Walzer's words, domination and tyranny.[35] Such a crossing into another sphere without a moral justification is like an illegal immigration so to speak, and therefore such an action is unjust. Nevertheless, there is an intrinsic relationship between nature and humankind because they are both integral to the great whole, UMUMTU. Because of their sacred character, such a relationship demands that humans ought to respect nature. Failure to give respect is tantamount to domination and tyranny.

Is there something else in common and different between humankind and nature, apart from the notion that they are interrelated because they are part of UMUMTU? Can humankind be considered a part of nature? Can humankind be considered different from nature or something superior to nature? Evolutionism has argued that humans have evolved from animals and that there is no way that humankind is superior to animals. Besides, science has revealed that the genome sequence of chimpanzees is more than 98 percent identical with that of human beings.[36] Hence, no radical difference exists between chimpanzees and man. Cardinal Christoph Schonborn thinks this argument is offensive:

> Man is derived from the realm of animals. In itself this is a problem neither for faith nor for reason as we shall see. What is offensive here is that he is supposed to reflect in some sense an unbroken line of development from Nature, so that between animals and men there is supposedly no discontinuity of nature, no metaphysical distinction. Man as a being with a mind, is seen as something not radically new in the great world of nature.[37]

This means that humankind is radically similar to nature in our physical composition and subject to the same chemical and physical laws. With the Copernican revolution, which has removed the earth from the center of the universe, how can humankind be considered the crown of creation, and why should humankind dominate creation?[38]

---

35. Again, Walzer believes that it is domination and tyranny if a man seeks to have sex with a woman because he is handsome or muscular. Feminists argue that it is unjust and tyrannical for a man to do so.

36. Schonborn, *Chance or Purpose*, 108.

37. Ibid., 108–9.

38. Ibid., 112.

Still, some critics have argued that the notion that humankind should dominate nature is biblical, and therefore it is morally justifiable to exploit nature to maximize the benefits of humankind. However, others have criticized this position of humankind's superiority or domination over nature by arguing that such a notion is a result of the distorted interpretation of the Genesis story of creation, which draws on the Priestly tradition.[39] Such an understanding has distorted the cosmic order leading to ecological catastrophe in the world. Citing the lives of the primitive hunter-gatherer tribes in the Amazon region, the Kalahari Desert, and the interior of Australia, Clobus argues that the integrity of creation is critical to human and nonhuman survival:

> The physical surrounding is experienced as an extension of the body. . . . The idea of human superiority or dominance over the surrounding world is foreign, even repugnant. It is considered to be self-evident that all creatures, sharing the same earth as mother, share its image. Likewise these people attribute to each plant and animal a purpose and an intrinsic value. The earth is home to many fellow-creatures who derive their right to be not from human beings but from the earth-mother which moulds them. It simply does not occur to them that human beings alone are created in the image of God or that they stand apart from and above the other creatures.[40]

With this kind of worldview, nature is understood to possess an intrinsic value, which exists independently of its utility or usefulness for humankind.[41] God's justice demands love and respect for all creation: both humankind and nature.

In an effort to offer the right interpretation of humankind's creation and the role we play in the whole of creation as shown in the biblical creation story, Schonborn suggests that love for humankind ought to be the highest priority over love for other creatures such as animals. Furthermore,

---

39. Clobus, *Environmental Care*, 30. It must be noted that there are two accounts of creation: The Yahwist biblical account of creation emphasizes humankind as a caretaker or a steward (Gen 2:9—3:24). The Priestly creation tradition emphasizes the notion that humankind is created in the image and likeness of God, and thus the tradition sets humankind above and apart from the rest of creation (Gen 1:1–3).

40. Ibid., 29–30.

41. Please refer to Mill's theory of the greatest principle of utility, presented in chapter 2 of this book.

Methodological Considerations for Constructing a Macrotheory of Justice 117

Schonborn insists that the way people express love for animals should not be in the same way they express love for other people.[42]

Marking World Peace Day in 1990, Pope John Paul II insisted that responsibility for the integrity of creation is critical to a peaceful society: "No peaceful society can afford to neglect either respect for life or the fact that there is integrity of creation."[43] Schonborn believes there is order of creation, which ought to be respected according to ranks:

> Yet it ought to be obvious that the order of creation is somehow distorted whenever animals are provided with luxuries while at the same time men are deprived of the most essential things. That does not mean that love for animals is something bad. There is simply an *ordo caritas*, an order in loving, which is in accordance with creation and which becomes immediately obvious when we are confronted with the case of parents who give everything possible to their pet dog but allow their children to starve. Or think of Rudolf Hob, the camp commandant at Auschwitz, who loved animals and was at the same time a cold-blooded mass murderer. People have already pointed out, a good many times, the painful fact that the animal protection lobby is given a better hearing in politics today than those who try to protect unborn children. The order of creation should provide a clear ranking of imperatives here. Yet even the notion of such a rank, a prioritizing, is understood by many people as if giving priority to the protection of human life before birth were an affront to quite justified efforts to protect animals.[44]

Schonborn believes that God's command to "subdue the earth" is "not a license for the unlimited plundering of creation."[45] Commenting on this similar subject is Clobus:

> The significance of this command, which has been misinterpreted so often, has undoubtedly contributed to the view that human beings sit astride nature like a rider taming a horse.... The temptation to dominate the world has been supported by another pillar of

---

42. Schonborn, *Chance or Purpose*, 152.

43. John Paul II, "Peace with God the Creator, Peace with All of Creation" (message for the celebration of the World Peace Day, 1990), http://www.vatican.va/holy_father/john_paul_ii/messages/peace/documents/hf_jp-ii_mes_19891208_xxiii-world-day-for-peace_en.html.

44. Ibid.

45. Ibid., 154.

our technological world, e.g., the Greco-Roman worldview so well expressed by Aristotle (*Politics* 1.8). 'For we must believe, first, that plants exist for the sake of animals, second, that all other animals exist for the sake of human beings.' The exploitation of natural resources on a massive scale by the West has been facilitated because people could take distance from the world, motivated to do so by their culture and religion. This gave them the freedom to dominate, control, and recreate nature in their own image. Faced with the near-reality of environmental ruin, we must now rediscover the creation tradition and the sense of immediacy of the natural world.[46]

Based on this distorted notion of creation and its negative impact on ecology, the study of an *umumtulogy* of justice is critical to shedding some light on effectives ways to resolve or prevent conflicts between humankind and nature, and thus restore abundant life in the universe.

THE UMUMTULOGY OF JUSTICE: CONFLICT RESOLUTION AND CONFLICT PREVENTION

It is a common understanding that a principle of justice deals with guiding and regulating ethical behavior and resolving and preventing conflicts of interests or conflicts of rights and duties in human society. The study of an umumtulogy of justice, however, has shown that justice not only deals with conflicts of interests among and between groups of people but that the umumtulogy of justice also deals with the way humankind ought to relate to nature. Studies have shown that some form of conflict or war, displacement of civilian populations, or death has occurred or is still occurring in those areas where there is drilling of crude oil, mining of diamonds or uranium, or lumbering or fishing activities. Between the 1980s and 1990s blood diamonds and black gold funded civil wars in Africa, such as in Angola between the MPLA government of Jose Eduardo dos Santos and the late Jonas Savimbi, leader of the UNITA guerrilla movement.[47] Similar events took place in the late 1990s in Sierra Leone's civil war, allegedly orchestrated with the help of the former president of Liberia, Charles Taylor. By looting and selling diamonds from Sierra Leone, Taylor was able to stay in power until he was forced to resign due to protracted

---

46. Clobus, Environmental Care, 41–42.
47. Meredith, *Fate of Africa*, 600–616.

civil war and political instability in Liberia. Liberia was also a center for laundering diamonds from other parts of African such as Angola.[48]

Geopolitical interests and globalization played a big part in the lives of the people in the Great Lakes region of Africa. The scramble for the natural resources like timber, diamonds, coltan, and gold by different political players in the Democratic Republic of Congo (DRC) has exacerbated tensions and led to conflicts, civil wars, political instability, economic stagnation, and abject poverty in the region.[49]

The demand for fish fillets from Tanzania in Europe has prevented small businessmen and women from earning a living. Such massive fishing in Lake Victoria in Tanzania has caused hopelessness and poverty in those communities around the lake. Consequently, some people are feeding on the pile of fish carcasses, and at times they compete with scavengers like big birds and other animals.[50]

It has been observed that because of global energy demand, there is a growing Chinese influence in Africa to tap its huge resources of crude oil while ignoring the sociopolitical and economic inequalities that run rampart, for example, among the people of western Darfur region of Sudan.[51] It has been alleged that the Chinese officials on the U.N. Security Council have been reluctant to join hands in imposing any sanctions to the Khartoum government in Sudan out of realpolitik. Such policy based on realpolitik or geopolitical interest has fueled tensions between governments and their people. The U.S. government, however, imposed economic sanctions on Sudan because of its involvement in committing genocide in the strife-stricken Darfur region of Sudan.[52]

The demand for crude oil in Nigeria is another realpolitik concern perpetuated by giant oil companies like Shell and others. This phenomenon has exacerbated tensions, conflicts, and wars, causing massive poverty and a slow death of a people in the Niger Delta region.[53]

In order to prevent conflicts between humankind and nature, justice requires that there be a balance between science, technology, develop-

---

48. Ibid., 572.
49. Ibid., 540–44.
50. Aina, "Mission of the Church," 246.
51. "Darfur Violence Increases as Peace Deadline Nears," *VOANews.com*, May 30, 2006, http://www.voanews.com/english/news/a-13-2006-05-30-voa29.html.
52. Ibid.
53. Ibid., 247.

ment, and the integrity of creation. Again, to resolve conflicts between humankind and nature, development ought to take into account the need for responsibility and accountability for actions that negatively impact the integrity of all of creation, including both humankind and nature. Self-conscious reflection, responsibility, and accountability for our actions are the basic elements that distinguish humans from nature (animals and others), as opposed to what Darwinian evolutionism would say.

I keep wondering what would be the contribution of Judeo-Christianity to the debate about the place of humankind in the universe. In response to scientific theories by Galileo Galilei and others that seem to dethrone the earth and, of course, humankind from being the center of the universe, the Second Vatican Council stated that humankind has been exalted above all creation and has a unique place and role in the universe. The right relationship among humankind, God and nature is brought to light when the importance of African cultural narratives, UMUMTU and ORUM, are considered in the study of justice and peace. Employing Christian social ethics and enriching them through the principles of an umumtulogy of justice can minimize, resolve, or prevent tensions, wars, and conflicts between humankind and nature in our world. To realize this task requires the concerted efforts of individuals, groups, and governmental and nongovernmental organizations.

THE UMUMTULOGY OF JUSTICE, SOLIDARITY, AND SUBSIDIARITY OF PEOPLES, CULTURES, NATIONS, AND RELIGIONS

The Umumtulogy of Justice and Secular Society

In African religion, the paradigm of the umumtulogy of justice inspires the sense of community, unity, solidarity, diversity, interrelationship, interdependence, integration, interconnection, and subsidiarity. The fruit of the umumtulogy of justice is abundant life: peace, wholeness, harmony, balance, order, happiness, fulfillment, and progress. Jewish justice, *sedaqah*, is described as fidelity to the demands of covenant relationship. Jesus Christ, through his death and resurrection, has brought about reconciliation, forgiveness, and peace, *shalom*, by restoring the ruptured relationship between God and the whole of creation: humankind and nature. Working for greater justice and peace is a fulfillment of the demands of *sedaqah*. Because in UMUMTU, humankind, nature, and God are intimately connected, justice does not only extend peace primarily to humankind, as Jewish justice has shown. In African religion, the umumtulogy of justice extends peace to the entire creation: humankind and nature. Therefore, UMUMTU is a better expression of justice than *sedaqah*. The African cultural narrative, UMUMTU, is not only significant to enriching the faith; it is also significant in promoting greater unity and solidarity among peoples, nations, cultures, and religions.

Rawls's principle of equality of the individual is an important contribution in promoting justice. To enjoy this liberal value, however, the concerted efforts of nations, peoples, cultures, and religions are critical, in contrast to the social contract of the abstract citizens in the method of the original position. Therefore, a real community of persons is critical to promoting the equality of all.

Redressing extreme inequalities among peoples may require more than just Rawls's difference principle. It has been alleged that the tax breaks for the rich in America did not ensure that benefits or profits trickled down to the worst-off. The rift between Wall Street and Main Street[54] has widened over the years. The 2008 global economic meltdown saw many people, most of who are from Main Street (not only in the rich nations but also in the developing ones), lose their savings, investments, homes, and jobs. Many people are convinced that the liberal and libertarian economic systems are to blame for the economic crisis, for the most part. To redress economic injustices would require a fundamental change in free-market economic policies. Going back to the drawing board to review policies is the way forward to redress economic injustices and restore peace. To succeed, solidarity among families, peoples, nations, cultures, and religions is critical. The paradigm of the umumtulogy of justice can inspire a sense of solidarity in resolving the crisis.

The libertarian view of justice focuses on the notion that society works best when each individual is responsible for his or her own choices and free from interference or coercion by the state. The role of the minimal

54. Wall Street is the location of the New York Stock Exchange in the United States. The expression *Main Street* as opposed to Wall Street does not denote a place, but rather it is applied to people who do not have the economic power to trade and benefit from the business transactions at the financial center at Wall Street. This expression was Obama's political slogan during the 2008 U.S. presidential campaign, and he addressed it to middle class America, which is struggling to survive, as opposed to Wall Street, which makes huge profits from trading at the New York Stock Exchange.

state is to protect and defend the freedom of its citizens and to adjudicate the fairness of transactions. However, individual choices in a free market economy have brought the world many economic disasters. In the light of the global economic meltdown, there is a need for government regulation of libertarian economic policies to stabilize the markets and put back the financial system in place. The paradigm of the umumtulogy of justice will instill a sense of the need for cooperation by governments and financial institutions the world over in dealing with the crisis.

Utilitarianism is an ethical theory that focuses with impartiality on the greatest happiness or satisfaction of all people. To achieve this goal requires not only the decision of one person; it requires mutual cooperation and contribution by peoples, nations, cultures, and religions. Most importantly, this cooperation is mostly critical to redressing the suffering and pain of most people who have been unjustly or unfairly deprived of abundant life. The paradigm of the umumtulogy of justice, which inspires the sense of community, solidarity, and subsidiarity, may be instrumental in achieving the greatest happiness for all with impartiality.

Communitarianism is an ethical-social theory with a focus on membership in a political community as the criterion for enjoying social goods. Hence, common humanity was not seen as the criterion for enjoying the social goods. In my view, membership in UMUMTU should become the criterion for enjoying the abundant life. Protecting social goods requires the cooperation and the concerted efforts of the political communities of nations, peoples, families, cultures, and religions. Jewish justice, *sedaqah*, makes similar calls for fidelity to the demands of this great and irreplaceable task.

Feminism focuses on the notion that society works best when the social, political, and economic barriers that have historically disempowered and disenfranchised women are acknowledged and abolished. In the interest of ensuring women's empowerment, the state must actively promote equality and dismantle historic barriers. Furthermore, religion and cultures have contributed in the oppression of women. To promote equality, empowerment, and inclusion of women both in the private and in the public sectors, the concerted efforts of states, peoples, nations, and organizations are critical in redressing injustices against women in the world. In addition, African feminism reflects the umumtulogy of justice, in advocating for the fact that sex, love, and procreation are inseparable, as opposed to some forms of Western feminism. The umumtulogy of justice inspires a sense of community and cooperation among peoples, social institutions, and nations, which is critical to redressing injustices against women.

Contemporary theories of justice focus mainly on human relationships mediated by goods. In African religion, the cultural narrative of justice, UMUMTU, regards nature as integral to UMUMTU, and therefore, it is a bearer of justice, in contrast to the Jewish cultural narrative of justice, *sedaqah*. Maintaining this type of relationship between humankind and nature is critical to promoting abundant life and social order in the world. Commenting on the impact of science at the time of the Renaissance of Galileo upon the understanding of the world as a wrong understanding of dominion is then cardinal Josef Ratzinger:

> At the time, a new kind of knowledge was being sought—not what things are, what constitutes their "nature," or, to put in another way, what their "logos" is, the divine idea that is being expressed in them—but rather what we can make out of them for ourselves. This approach to reality is called "power knowledge."[55]

A distortion of such an order through science, technology, and poverty, particularly in the developing world, causes injustices against nature and leads to disaster in the world. Redressing injustices against nature will reverse this trend. The paradigm of an umumtulogy of justice is a source of inspiration for families, peoples, nations, and cultures to take responsibility and protect the integrity of nature.

The Umumtulogy of Justice and Ecumenism

Many religious scholars have expressed the idea that African religion is a tribal religion and therefore it lacks the legitimacy to be considered equal to other world religions.[56] This criticism is based on the notion that African religion lacks a sacred text, is unrevealed, and does not carry out a converting process.[57] It has to be clear that the oral tradition precedes the written text, as Judaism and Christianity have shown.[58] Tribal religions such as Buddhism and Confucianism do not generally proselytize,

---

55. Schonborn, *Chance or Purpose*, 155.
56. Magesa, *African Religion*, 30.
57. Ibid., 30–31.
58. Ibid., 30.

and yet they are considered world religions.[59] Responding to the question of whether or not the African religion is a revealed religion, the question is not so much about doctrine but rather it is first and foremost about a way of life. This means that in Africa, religion and ethics are inseparable.[60] Because the African cultural narrative, UMUMTU, has already been seen earlier as significant to a deeper understanding of justice and peace, one should no longer doubt, as it was doubted in the recent past, that African religion has no place on the world stage.

Because of what the paradigm of the umumtulogy of justice stands for, the call for the solidarity of all world religions to embark upon a decisive action could provide a solution to the current problem of ecological crisis. All world religions, such as Buddhism, Judaism, Christianity, Hinduism, Islam, and African religion, have something in common: the strong sense of interrelation in all of creation as well as a belief in the sacred character of creation. It is this common ground that should encourage these religions to dialogue with each other and with science in the spirit of solidarity and resolve to seek a lasting solution to the ecological crisis.

The interconnection between religion and creation was quite significant during the twenty-fifth anniversary of the World Wide Fund for Nature, during which the representatives of the world religions made declarations. Buddhism maintains the interconnection of all reality.[61] Christianity maintains that all creation is good, that order and harmony exist in creation, and that humankind has been entrusted with the responsibility to care for creation.[62] Hinduism believes in the presence of the divine and that humankind is an integral part of creation.[63] Islam is all about peace with humankind and with nature. Peace, therefore, is a fruit of the submission of our will with the will of God. Nature is given to humankind with trust to maintain order and harmony in the universe.[64]

---

59. Ibid., 32.
60. Ibid., 33.
61. Clobus, *Environmental Care*, 30–31.
62. Ibid., 31.
63. Ibid.
64. Ibid., 31–32.

Jewish religion believes that humankind ought to play a central role in creation in keeping with what each creature is intended to be.[65]

Nevertheless, the world has not been a better place to live in despite the presence of all these rich religious beliefs and heritage. Ecological crisis looms large in the homes or areas of the world religions, ranging from the Middle East to Asia to Africa. So, then, what has gone wrong there? Do you think that science and technology have turned a blind eye on religion? Or perhaps both science and religion are in conflict with each other? Can harmony exist between the two? As Ratzinger noted, the problem is rooted in the right understanding of the character of nature, a notion that brings together nature and religion. According to African religion, the paradigm of the umumtulogy of justice is a bridge between humankind and nature and between creation and God. In the spirit of subsidiarity, inspired by UMUMTU and ORUM, all these religions have a moral responsibility to dialogue with science and technology to restore justice and peace in the universe. Through the spirit of ecumenism, world religious leaders must gather together to dialogue with the international community and other organizations, as they did during the September 1986 assembly in Assisi when they shared constructive ideas to resolve and prevent unnecessary conflict, wars, and injustices against nature.

The study of the umumtulogy of justice offers the understanding that humankind—the unborn, the living, and the living dead—are the claimants of justice and that nature is integral to the community of UMUMTU and ORUM. The abundant life, the fruit of justice, involves the fulfillment of both the negative and positive duties of justice, as opposed to contemporary theories of justice, which lay more emphasis on the negative duties of justice than on the positive duties of justice.

In the contemporary world, quality of life is often equated to quantity, but with the study of macrojustice, however, it has been seen that quality of life is all about right relationships, as in *sedaqah* and UMUMTU. Furthermore, because justice is often restricted to human relationships, humankind (not including the unborn and the living dead) is the sole bearer of justice claims, and these contemporary theories fall short of regarding nature (both animate and inanimate) as the bearer of justice claims.

---

65. Ibid., 32.

Peace is the fruit of right relationships with God, humankind, and nature through Christ, the justice of God. This study of macrojustice contributes to the understanding, promotion, and protection of abundant life for all, and thus it offers a window of opportunity to create a spirituality of justice and peace as recommended by the 2002 AMECEA Bishops' assembly on "Deeper Evangelization in the Third Millennium" as well as to develop an ecological ethics as recommended by the U.S. Catholic Bishops' 2002 pastoral letter, "Economic Justice for All." The paradigm of the umumtulogy of justice calls for protecting humankind and nature, the bearers of justice. For such a project to succeed, the concerted efforts of all peoples, nations, cultures, institutions, and religions are required. Fulfilling the demands of the umumtulogy of justice will be beneficial not only to the present generation of humanity, but also to the future of all humankind—unborn, living, and living dead—and all of creation.

General Conclusion

It may seem that the journey has come to an end. Or, perhaps, it has just started to break new grounds. The quest for a new understanding of justice is still an ongoing process as long as humanity and its habitat are around. The attempt to critique the contemporary theories of justice, the task of part 1, was prompted by the fact that the successes of such theories have to be appreciated and promoted. Their shortcomings, however, are a blessing in disguise and have become a stepping stone to furthering a better knowledge of justice and peace.

Biblical justice and African cultural narratives of justice, UMUMTU and ORUM, are a good source for the new understanding of justice. From these two different social milieus, part 2 retrieved certain insights for the construction of a new understanding of justice. One basic insight, the leitmotif, is the ethical and moral value of relationships as fidelity to the demands of justice claims. Fulfilling these demands ensures that the dignity of humankind and nature is protected and leads to the enjoyment of the abundant life. The theme of relationships in the spheres of both humankind and nature dominated this study, which was seen as critical to enjoying abundant life and as the fruit of integrating different threads or ingredients of the community called UMUMTU.

In the light of the African cultural narratives of justice, UMUMTU and ORUM, and the biblical narrative of justice, *sedaqah*, five principles have been retrieved as the framework for constructing a new theory of justice, the task of part 3. Through this structure, humankind, nature, and

God were seen as the bearers of justice claims as opposed to the claims of contemporary theories of justice, in which humans are the sole bearers of justice claims. Most importantly, the study established that positive justice and positive duties of justice are critical to satisfying these claims, as opposed to the contemporary theories' emphasis on negative justice and negative duties over positive justice and positive duties. Because the umumtulogy of justice inspires the need for relationships within both secular and religious communities and the need for the solidarity of all humanity, satisfying the demands for macrojustice requires the solidarity of all peoples, cultures, nations, organizations, and religions. In the spirit of ecumenism, African religion, through the umumtulogy of justice, in conjunction with other world religions, can be instrumental to offering a solution for protecting the whole of creation: humankind and nature.

Bibliography

Aina, Raymond O. "The Mission of the Church in Africa Today: Reconciliation?" *AFER* 50, nos. 3 and 4 (2008) 218–65.
Betsworth, Roger G. *Social Ethics: An Examination of American Moral Traditions.* Louisville, KY: Westminster John Knox, 1990.
Cahill, Sowle L. "Feminism and Christian Ethics." In *Freeing Theology: The Essentials of Theology in Feminist Perspective*, edited by Catherine Mowry LaCugna, 211–31. San Francisco: Harper, 1993.
Clobus, Rob. *Environmental Care: A Possible Way to Restore God's Image.* Spearhead Monographs 122. Eldoret, Kenya: AMECEA Gabba, 1992.
Curran, Charles. *Catholic Social Teaching 1891–Present: A Historical, Theological, and Ethical Analysis.* Washington, DC: Georgetown University Press, 2002.
"Deeper Evangelization in the Third Millennium: A Challenge to AMECEA." AMECEA 14th Plenary. Eldoret: AMECEA Gabba. *AFER* 44, nos. 5 and 6 (2002) 264–82.
Donahue, John R. "Biblical Perspectives on Justice." In *The Faith That Does Justice: Examining the Christian Sources of Social Change*, edited by John C. Haughey, 68–109. New York: Paulist Press, 1977.
Farley, Margaret A. "Feminist Theology and Bioethics." In *Feminist Theological Ethics*, edited by Lois K. Daly. Louisville, KY: Westminster John Knox, 1994.
Lebacqz, Karen. *Justice in an Unjust World.* Minneapolis, MN: Fortress, 2007.
———. *Six Theories of Justice: Perspectives from Philosophical and Theological Ethics.* Minneapolis, MN: Augsburg, 1986.
McFadden, Patricia. "The State of Feminism in Africa Today." *News from the Nordic Africa Institute*, no. 2 (2000) http://www.nai.uu.se/publications/news/archives/002mcfadden/
Magesa, Laurenti. *African Religion: The Moral Traditions of Abundant Life.* Nairobi, Kenya: Paulines, 1977.
Meredith, Martin. *The Fate of Africa: A History of Fifty Years of Independence.* New York: PublicAffairs, 2005.
Mill, Stuart J. *Utilitarianism and On Liberty.* Edited by Mary Warnock. Malden, MA: Blackwell, 2003.
Msoka, Gabriel A. *Basic Human Rights and the Humanitarian Crises in Sub-Saharan Africa: Ethical Reflections.* Eugene, OR: Pickwick Publications, 2007.
———. "Cosmotheandrization of Human Rights: A Focus on Refugees and Internally Displaced Persons in Africa." *AFER* 49, nos. 1 and 2 (2007) 62–96.
Nozick, Robert. *Anarchy, State, and Utopia.* New York: Basic Books, 1974.
Okin, Susan. M. *Justice, Gender, and the Family.* New York: Basic Books, 1989.

———. "Inequalities between the Sexes in Different Cultural Contexts." In *Women, Culture and Development*, edited by Martha C. Nussbaum and Jonathan Glover, 275–94. Oxford: Clarendon, 1995.

Oduyoye, Amba M. "Feminist Theology in an African Perspective." In *Paths of African Theology*, edited by Rosino Gibellini, 166–80. Maryknoll, NY: Orbis, 1994.

Rawls, John. *A Theory of Justice*. Cambridge, MA: Belknap Press of Harvard University Press, 1971.

Schonborn, Christoph. C. *Chance or Purpose: Creation and a Rational Faith*. Edited by Hubert Philip Weber. San Francisco: Ignatius, 2007.

Schreiter, Robert. *The New Catholicity: Theology between the Global and the Local*. Maryknoll, NY: Orbis, 2000.

Segers, Mary C. "Feminism, Liberalism, and Catholicism." In *Catholicism and Liberalism*, edited Douglas Bruce R. and David Hollenbach. New York: Cambridge University Press, 1994.

Ssentumbwe, Pius M. "Peace: A Crucial Mission of the Holy See and United Nations." *AFER* 50, nos. 3 and 4 (2008) 197–217.

Synod of Bishops. "Justice in the World." 1971. Reprinted in *Catholic Social Thought: The Documentary Heritage*, edited by David J. O'Brien and Thomas A. Shannon, 288–300. Maryknoll, NY: Orbis, 2001.

Tong, Rosemarie. *Feminist Approaches to Bioethics: Theoretical Reflections and Practical Applications*. Boulder, CO: West View, 1997.

Traina, Cristina. *Feminist Ethics and Natural Law: The End of the Anathemas*. Washington, DC: Georgetown University Press, 1999.

U.S. Catholic Bishops. "Economic Justice for All." 1986. Reprinted in *Catholic Social Thought: The Documentary Heritage*, edited by David J. O'Brien and Thomas A. Shannon, 572–664. Maryknoll, NY: Orbis, 2001.

Walzer, Michael. *Spheres of Justice: A Defense of Pluralism and Equality*. New York: Basic Books, 1983.

Young, Iris M. *Justice and the Politics of Difference*. Princeton, NJ: Princeton University Press, 1990.

www.ingramcontent.com/pod-product-compliance
Lightning Source LLC
Chambersburg PA
CBHW071858160426
43197CB00013B/2521